To John —

Best
wishes

Barry Kaye

YOU BUY
YOU DIE
IT PAYS!

Testimonials
from Previous Works
By Barry Kaye

Mr. Kaye's books answer clearly and concisely the "what to do" and "how to do" type questions that haunt clients in the areas of estate and financial planning. If true genius can be defined as the ability to reduce complex problems to easily understandable concepts, Mr. Kaye has achieved that status.

Richard Creange
New York, NY

Mr. Kaye's concepts are so extraordinary they have completely changed the way I use life insurance in my estate planning.

Mark Papalia, CLU, ChFC, CFP • Papalia Financial Services, Inc.
Danville, PA

Barry Kaye is inspiring! Of all the seminars I have attended, he is the best I have ever seen.

Michael Hebner, First Vice President • Roney & Co.
Flint, MI

The life insurance industry owes Mr. Kaye an immense debt of gratitude for placing the significance of life insurance in the forefront of people's financial and estate plans through his creative and personal investment where the industry has been the beneficiary at large.

Bijan Nahai • Nahai Insurance Services
Beverly Hills, CA

After 30 years I have come to the conclusion that for income, estate and gift tax purposes Barry's wealth creation and optimization methods really work and fully deliver on promises.
> Ralph S. Adorno, CLU and Associates
> *New York, NY*

Barry is right! After 30 years with the Internal Revenue Service, Estate and Gift Tax Department, I am convinced that the best estate planning is *life insurance planning,* carefully implemented to avoid estate taxation.
> Stephen L. Diamond, J.D.
> *Los Angeles, CA*

Mr. Kaye, you are an inspiration to my business and me. The conviction with which you practice invigorates the entire industry.
> Lynne Rosenberg-Kidd • Innovative Solutions • Transamerica
> *Los Angeles, CA*

Thank you Mr. Kaye! Your systems and methods have changed my life.
> Mitchell Cohen
> *Encino, CA*

Mr. Kaye, you amaze me! Thank you for showing me the power.
> Jesse Savage • American Express • IDS
> *Las Vegas, NV*

Barry, you are the greatest! Because of you I have completely changed the way I look at life insurance.
> Bob Kersting, Jr. • John Hancock Agency
> *Phoenix, AZ*

Barry, your innovative concepts and your wealth transfer techniques are absolutely incredible. You are the ultimate maverick in a sea of conventional wisdom. Your conviction and passion are truly evangelical.
> Martin Greenberg, Chairman • Total Financial & Insurance Services
> *Los Angeles, CA*

Mr. Kaye, you're my hero! I was an accountant who didn't know. Now I see the light.
> David Owens, CPA
> *Readfield*, ME

Books by Barry Kaye

$2,700,000 In My First Year (1963)

How to Save a Fortune on Your Life Insurance (1980)

Save a Fortune on Your Estate Taxes (1990)

Die Rich and Tax Free (1994)

Live Rich (1996)

The Investment Alternative (1997)

Die Rich 2 (2000)

You Buy, You Die, It Pays! (2007)

YOU BUY YOU DIE IT PAYS!

Life Insurance:
It Doesn't Pay to Die Without It!

30 AMAZING CONCEPTS

Dr. Barry Kaye, CLU

FHA PRESS

A Checklist: Insuring Your Family's Future as reprinted from the
August 2006 issue of *Smart Business Broward/Palm Beach*.
Copyright © 2006
Smart Business Network Inc.

ISBN 10: 1-930-286-01-5
ISBN 13: 978-1-930286-01-6

Printed in the United States of America

06 07 08 09 10   5 4 3 2 1

Dedication

This is the ultimate compilation of all my books, ideas and new concepts. I can do no more than rededicate my total efforts to all who have motivated, inspired and supported me over the past 45 years of my career.

My special thanks to my children, Fern, Alan and Howard, who have been with me since the beginning of their careers and have made it all worthwhile. My long-time associates at Barry Kaye Associates, and more recently National Financial Partners have also provided an excellent support system.

As usual, I dedicate this book to my beloved lifetime partner, Carole, who has made my life beautiful, meaningful and possible, and without whom there would be no Barry Kaye.

Contents

From the Publisher

The author of this book describes many situations that he had available to him at the time it was being written. Without knowledge of your specific requirements, the publisher and author disclaim any liability for loss incurred by use of direct or indirect application of the material contained herein. These ideas and concepts are only a starting point. Only the proper professionals can determine the complete suitability for you, as well as to consummate the proper implementation of these methods for optimizing and preserving your wealth for your family. Any change in the basic assumptions as described will alter the specific results and returns. However, in most cases, the results still will be superior to those using other approaches. Naturally, all results also are limited by the assumed solvency of the company or consortium of companies that you use.

Since any reference to an internal rate of return must be based on an assumed interest rate and period of time, there can be no such comparison made, due to the uncertainty of when death will occur. In all cases, the author has recommended diversification of his client's portfolio, and in most cases used less than 10% of the client's assets in doing so. Since he never proposes any financial action that would adversely affect his client's lifestyle, the internal rate of return is irrelevant in what these ideas and concepts will provide. Most of the concepts described in this book apply to individuals worth $5 million or more.

You should contact your attorney for the implementation of any legal papers, such as trust documents, that may be necessary for carrying out these ideas. Trust officers can further provide you with the necessary information relative to these documents.

Previous books by the author may go into more detail on any concept presented herein, but the main purpose of this book is to explain, simplistically and succinctly, the author's 30 amazing concepts.

This book expresses the ideas of the author, but not necessarily the views of National Financial Partners, the publisher or any insurance company.

For a better understanding of the concepts and approaches discussed in this book, please see Chapter 14 for an explanation of terms and technical approaches.

Introduction

I am in my 79th year by the time this is published. I have been in the insurance business for 45 years, more than half of my life. During my career, I have led 15 different companies. I was a catalyst in the creation of last-to-die survivorship insurance in 1963. In the last 5 years I created the concept of saving substantial premiums by funding policies on a life expectancy basis. I have written 7 books on this subject, and I am a professor at the Barry Kaye School of Finance, Insurance and Economics at Florida Atlantic University (FAU), where I received my honorary doctorate. I am also responsible for creating the Barry Kaye Institute of Insurance in Philanthropy at FAU. This is the 8th book I have written on insurance and estate optimization.

Over the past 4½ decades I have learned, observed and determined without question the right way and the wrong way, the dos and the don'ts of proper planning to optimize your estate at death. Mistakes are made constantly. Advisors with antiquated biases still do not use all the options available and therefore many clients are ill advised. These are very costly mistakes and can wreak havoc, devastating a lifetime's work and estate.

It is with this in mind that I have determined the time has come to write another book. There is a wrong way and a right way to maximize an estate. These are simple facts. The numbers will prove themselves. They will either be smaller or larger. Your heirs and favorite charities will either have more or less. This will be irrefutable. There may be a cost to accomplish these objectives, but if you have enough money to support your lifestyle and the rest is ultimately for your heirs and favorite charities, why not take some money from the future and optimize the ultimate assets? Isn't there a cost and expense for any kind of estate planning done or undone? The question simply is which produces the best results.

Who would be better equipped to write this than someone with the 45-year experience and the credentials I have stated above?

The format for this book will include a right and wrong way for each subject. Wrong is wrong, but in some cases wrong may represent conventional wisdom. However, the right way will always represent the more productive approach. This book is intended to show the best way at the inception of the plan and does not cover the potential of an alternate program that may or may not come to be. Obviously there can be diversification and you still might use some of the previously accepted conventional wisdom approaches. These programs use life insurance policies and therefore are limited to the maximums that can be purchased. They are further limited by the health of the parties involved. This may make it necessary to use or augment your plans with the existing conventional wisdom when you can no longer use the better insurance approaches.

Wrong is only wrong when there is a better way. It can become the only way to proceed if there are no alternatives or surrogate insureds available. You are further limited by the total amount of insurance of approximately $250 million that can be purchased from a consortium of insurance companies. I have written in the first part of this book about 6 major concepts and more than 24 secondary ideas that should make an extraordinary difference in the final totals. With the necessary caveats stated and accepted you can now proceed to learn how to die richer.

YOU BUY
YOU DIE
IT PAYS!

CHAPTER 1

Advanced Basics of
Wealth Preservation

Subject to new tax law that is constantly in formation, you and your spouse each may gift $12,000 to as many people as you wish yearly. In this manner 3 children and 7 grandchildren will allow total annual tax free gifts of $240,000 to your heirs or an irrevocable trust. This will reduce your estate substantially each year. Since all planning is for death, you can purchase a last-to-die survivorship insurance policy that guarantees to pay approximately $24 million at your deaths (based on male and female age 65). The actual deaths that create the need for this insurance creates the proceeds. Since your yearly gifts eliminate assets from your estate that would have been taxed in approximately a 50% estate tax bracket, you could say that the $240,000 yearly gifts are not only gift-tax free but also effectively tax deductible.

In this manner, buying life insurance, you not only have reduced your taxable estate by $240,000 yearly but you have created $24 million tax free. This is equivalent to creating a $48 million pre-tax asset in a 50% estate tax bracket. What other investment alternative can produce a $48 million asset for $240,000 a year; certainly not stock or real estate. What's wrong with a little diversification on a guaranteed basis?

If you use life expectancy funding techniques, a concept I developed over the past 5 years, you can even optimize the amount of insurance you can purchase for the same price. You use your life expectancy of approximately age 85. If you live past 85 you have the opportunity to pay additional premiums to continue the policy with no further medical requirements. The same $240,000 yearly will buy approximately $48 million of tax free insurance or the equivalent of creating a $96 million pre-tax asset. If only life insurance had been understood all these years by those who sold it or those advisors who advised against it or bought it in limited quantities, or by the public.

EXAMPLE 1

Husband and Wife Each Have a Tax Free Annual Gift of $12,000	3 Children 7 Grandchildren Husband and Wife Can Give $240,000 Annually to Irrevocable Trust	Trust Purchases Up to $48 Million on a Life Expectancy Basis
Net Cost $6,000	Net Cost $120,000/year	

Effectively Remove $240,000 a Year from Your Estate
At Death It Becomes $24 Million to $48 Million
ESTATE TAX FREE!

The above stated information was based on your annual exemptions. You and your spouse are also allowed a one-time lifetime exemption of $1 million each for a total of $2 million. Using the same techniques previously described here, a last-to-die survivorship, one-payment policy is bought for approximately $14 million (based on male and female age 65). Transferring $2 million out of the estate to the heirs or an irrevocable trust produces $14 million tax free. This is equivalent to a $28 million pre-tax asset. How else can this be produced, guaranteed at death?

If a life expectancy policy is used, one payment of $2 million can purchase a $50 million death benefit tax free, equivalent to a $100 million pre-tax asset.

EXAMPLE 2		
Husband and Wife Each Have a Tax Free Lifetime Gift of $1,000,000	Husband and Wife Can Give $2,000,000 Once to Irrevocable Trust	Trust Purchases Up to $50 Million on a Life Expectancy Basis

One-Time Payment of $2,000,000 Can Become Up to $50 Million ESTATE TAX FREE!

Now that you understand the basic numbers, assets created and tax consequences, you can apply these policies to create the various money saving, wealth creation and preservation techniques that I have developed over the years.

All examples were based on using available annual or lifetime exemptions. If your exemptions have already been used you will find that paying gift taxes on additional or larger gifts will have minimal effect on the cost efficiency and substantial profits to be gained using these approaches. Furthermore, leverage can be achieved by borrowing the premiums and paying annual interest, which may be tax deductible and in many instances less than the actual annual premium.

CHAPTER 2

Double, Duplicate and Recreate Assets

Using the information provided in Chapter 1 you are now ready to apply this to your own situation. Remember, knowledge without application is worthless. If you do it the right way, the only estate plan you may ever need is life insurance.

Let's recreate your assets and actually double them. This will put you in a position to give your estate away twice; discount your estate tax costs; increase your exemptions many times; increase wealth for your children and grandchildren; optimize what you leave to charity; and increase up to 50 times what you leave from your IRA, pension and profit sharing plans. Using these techniques you may also recover any investment losses in the stock market or real estate; maximize business or investment returns; convert debts to assets and recover any taxes paid.

CHAPTER 3

Give Your Estate Away Twice

Let's suppose your estate is worth $20 million after all exemptions. After estate taxes of approximately 50%, your net estate is worth $10 million. You make an $800,000 gift to an irrevocable trust that purchases a life expectancy last-to-die survivorship policy on you and your spouse for $20 million. This results at your deaths in your heirs receiving $20 million, or 100% of your estate free of gift, income and estate taxes. The 100% balance of your estate, $20 million, is donated at your deaths to charity or your own foundation. In this way you have given your estate away twice; $20 million to your heirs and $20 million to charity for a total of $40 million, or 200% of your assets, instead of your heirs receiving $10 million for a total of 50%. At the bottom line you have quadrupled your net estate. Your heirs can also become trustees of your foundation and receive yearly trustee fees.

I have found no better way to achieve these results; therefore this is right. Any other technique is wrong unless it can out-produce the above bottom line.

(See example 3 on the following page.)

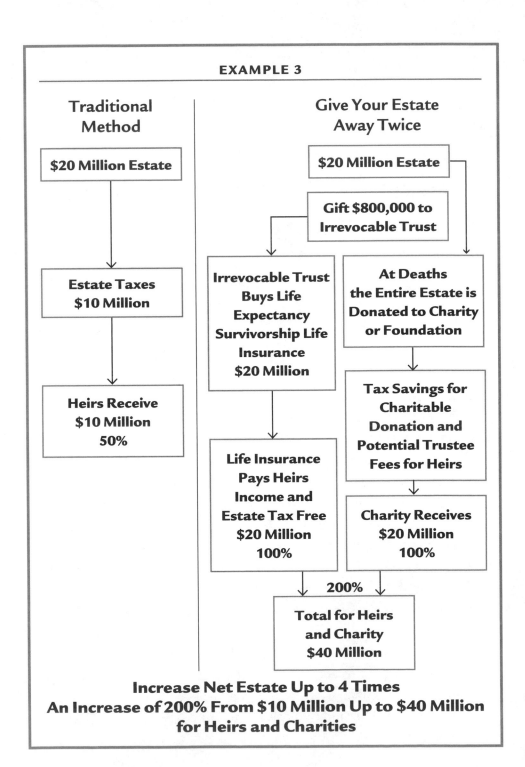

EXAMPLE 3

Traditional Method

$20 Million Estate

Estate Taxes
$10 Million

Heirs Receive
$10 Million
50%

Give Your Estate Away Twice

$20 Million Estate

Gift $800,000 to Irrevocable Trust

Irrevocable Trust Buys Life Expectancy Survivorship Life Insurance $20 Million

At Deaths the Entire Estate is Donated to Charity or Foundation

Life Insurance Pays Heirs Income and Estate Tax Free $20 Million 100%

Tax Savings for Charitable Donation and Potential Trustee Fees for Heirs

Charity Receives $20 Million 100%

200%

Total for Heirs and Charity $40 Million

**Increase Net Estate Up to 4 Times
An Increase of 200% From $10 Million Up to $40 Million for Heirs and Charities**

CHAPTER 4

Increase Your Exemptions from $2 Million to $100 Million

Using the same ideas already described, you and your spouse can increase your $1 million exemptions from $2 million to $100 million. An exemption means you pay no tax on the first $2 million of your assets. If you could effectively increase your exemptions to $100 million from the current $2 million, your heirs would save 50% taxes ($49 million). If you transferred $2 million gift tax free to an irrevocable trust, the trust could purchase a $50 million life expectancy last-to-die survivorship insurance policy on your lives. When you both die the policy will pay the $50 million tax free death benefit to the trust, which will then effectively pay the estate tax. Since none of the taxes were paid from your own previous assets you have effectively increased your exemption to $100 million. Your only cost to pay the $50 million tax was the one-payment $2 million insurance premium.

If your estate was $20 million you would need only $400,000 to purchase the $10 million necessary to increase your effective exemption to $20 million. Do you wish to pay taxes of $10 million (retail wrong way) or insurance premiums of $400,000 (wholesale right way)?

There is even a more cost efficient way to pay for this increased exemption. Use the leverage of a loan against your stock and bond portfolio or your real estate. Instead of paying $400,000, borrow it and pay approximate interest of $28,000 a year to create $10 million. Where else can you pay $28,000 a year to create $10 million, while the interest may be tax deductible if structured properly. When the loan is paid off at death, Uncle Sam effectively pays off half of the loan, costing your heirs only $200,000.

If you wanted to increase your exemption to $100 million using the leverage plan it would cost only $140,000 interest yearly. Where else can you pay $140,000 a year to create $50 million?

(See example 4 on the following page.)

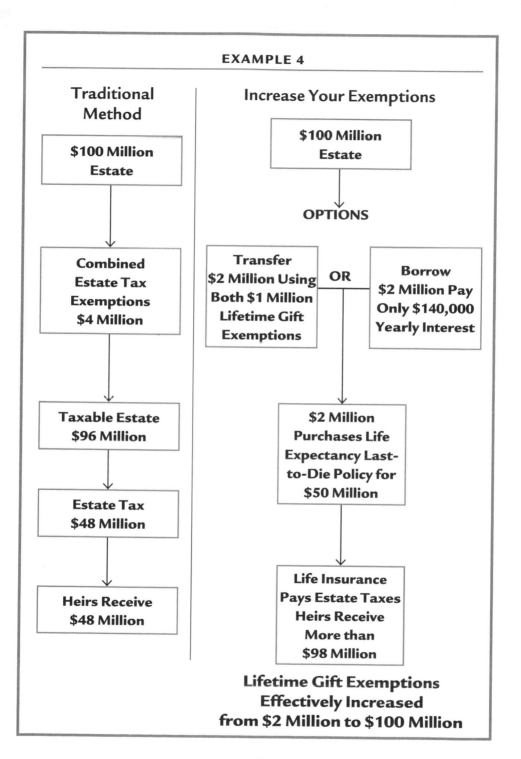

EXAMPLE 4

Traditional Method

$100 Million Estate

↓

Combined Estate Tax Exemptions $4 Million

↓

Taxable Estate $96 Million

↓

Estate Tax $48 Million

↓

Heirs Receive $48 Million

Increase Your Exemptions

$100 Million Estate

↓

OPTIONS

Transfer $2 Million Using Both $1 Million Lifetime Gift Exemptions   **OR**   Borrow $2 Million Pay Only $140,000 Yearly Interest

↓

$2 Million Purchases Life Expectancy Last-to-Die Policy for $50 Million

↓

Life Insurance Pays Estate Taxes Heirs Receive More than $98 Million

Lifetime Gift Exemptions Effectively Increased from $2 Million to $100 Million

CHAPTER 5

Discount Your Estate Tax Costs

You should have noticed by now that each chapter of this book is different and accomplishes a different objective. However, all of the techniques to achieve those objectives are very similar. As an author I should worry about the redundancy but I am well aware of the absolute necessity to reinforce these ideas. The mindset for most people is so bad when it comes to insurance that they just don't get it. It is imperative to learn and understand that life insurance is not what it is but what it does. Most life insurance agents don't understand this, nor do advisors and their clients. Life insurance isn't about policies, premiums and small print. It's simply about optimizing and maximizing the bottom line. Nothing in nearly every case will produce a better return at death, since death is guaranteed.

If you are worth $10 million at death after all exemptions, the approximate tax is $5 million. This can be paid with your liquid dollars or a last-to-die survivorship life insurance policy for an annual premium of approximately $50,000 or a one-time premium of $750,000. If you used a life expectancy policy the one-time premium could be as little as $200,000. If you borrowed the $200,000 the only annual outlay would be the interest of approximately $14,000 a year, possibly tax deductible. The choice is up to you. Your heirs pay $5 million at your deaths or you pay as little as $14,000 a year until your deaths.

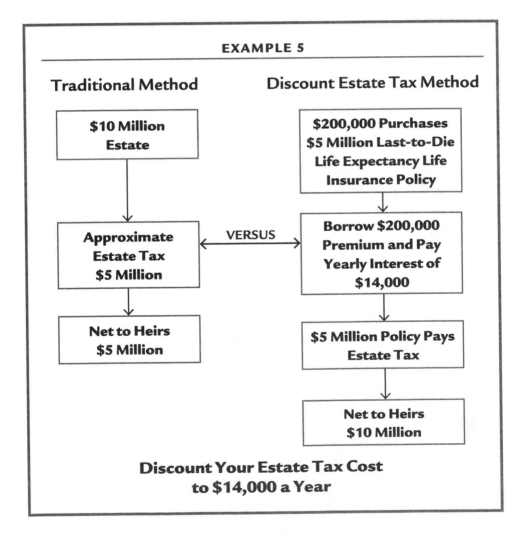

EXAMPLE 5

Traditional Method	Discount Estate Tax Method
$10 Million Estate	**$200,000 Purchases $5 Million Last-to-Die Life Expectancy Life Insurance Policy**
Approximate Estate Tax $5 Million VERSUS	**Borrow $200,000 Premium and Pay Yearly Interest of $14,000**
Net to Heirs $5 Million	**$5 Million Policy Pays Estate Tax**
	Net to Heirs $10 Million

Discount Your Estate Tax Cost to $14,000 a Year

As in most of the examples found in this book, the numbers can be increased or decreased to fit your specific requirements. The next example uses a $100 million estate and follows the same steps as above. The premium will increase proportionate to $2 million and if borrowed will cost only $140,000 to provide your heirs with $50 million at your deaths.

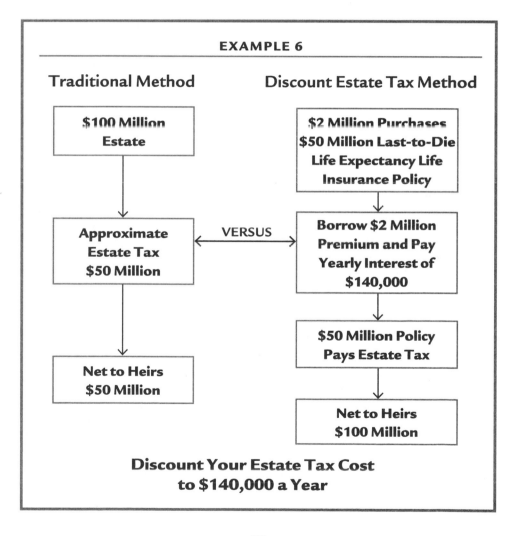

EXAMPLE 6

Traditional Method

Discount Estate Tax Method

$100 Million Estate

$2 Million Purchases $50 Million Last-to-Die Life Expectancy Life Insurance Policy

Approximate Estate Tax $50 Million

VERSUS

Borrow $2 Million Premium and Pay Yearly Interest of $140,000

$50 Million Policy Pays Estate Tax

Net to Heirs $50 Million

Net to Heirs $100 Million

Discount Your Estate Tax Cost to $140,000 a Year

CHAPTER 6

Create Optimal Wealth for Your Children, Grandchildren and Charity

If there were no estate taxes, exemptions or tax discounts you should still buy life insurance as a commodity. It is a further method of diversification and certainly an excellent investment alternative. It is a guaranteed way to leave substantial additional assets, since death is guaranteed. Only extra money in excess of what is required to support one's lifestyle should be used to pay the premiums to purchase life insurance. Assets in excess of your lifestyle needs are for your heirs anyway, so why not take some of these future monies and use them for insurance that guarantees extra money when passed on at death?

Insurance can be bought on individuals, or last-to-die policies on two people can be used. By using life expectancy leveraged policies the premiums can be brought to the lowest outlay for maximum coverage. The following chart shows the cost and extent of last-to-die financed life expectancy insurance at 6% interest.

EXAMPLE 7			
Death Benefit	One-Pay Premium	Yearly Premium	Yearly Interest
$1,000,000	$40,000	$4,000	$2,400
$5,000,000	$200,000	$20,000	$12,000
$10,000,000	$400,000	$40,000	$24,000
$25,000,000	$1,000,000	$100,000	$60,000
$50,000,000	$2,000,000	$200,000	$120,000
$100,000,000	$4,000,000	$400,000	$240,000

For as little as $2,400 a year you can create $1 million for your heirs and charity. The gifts to charity could also be tax deductible. Depending on your level of assets and objectives you could spend $120,000 yearly and create $50 million. Finally, where else can you put $240,000 yearly and create $100 million? Once again the bottom line proves this approach to be one of the best methods to diversify and optimize your assets at your deaths.

While you have to die for the asset to be available, insurance in force is guaranteed at death and death is guaranteed. Insurance is nothing more than money and will spend the same way as stock, real estate or any other asset. Life insurance: the ultimate asset; it really doesn't pay to die without it. You buy; you die; it pays!

CHAPTER 7

Maximize Real Estate and Stock Gains; Minimize Stock Market and Other Investment Losses

As one gets older there is a tendency toward selling a business or other investments in order to do proper estate planning. If a small percentage of any sale proceeds is directed toward life insurance it can substantially increase the return and profit realized on those assets. If you sold a business for approximately $5 million and used 10% of the assets, $500,000, to purchase second-to-die survivorship life insurance, you would buy about a $3 million policy. This would bring the total value of your business sale to $7.5 million at your death. This represents a 50% increase in the original sale price.

Obviously these figures work at any price. If you sold the same business for $50 million and used the same 10%, $5 million, you would buy a $30 million policy. This brings the total value of your business sale to $75 million at your death, still representing a 50% increase in the original sale price.

You can apply these same principles to any stock, real estate or other investment and produce the same results. A $100 million sale could produce $150 million, and $200 million could produce $300 million. Since you are usually selling these assets at the latter part of your life and you won't need all of them to support your lifestyle, why are you leaving this extra money on the table?

You can also structure these policies to your great tax advantage, paying estate taxes only on the initial premiums and not the greater death benefit. All taxes can be legally avoided if you have not used your allowable exemptions.

Smaller or larger percentages can be used in accordance with your own objectives. I have recommended this simple approach for many years and I am astonished how infrequently it is recommended by other advisors. If a client really understood this, there would be no question that any other technique or just not using it is wrong. It is the only way to optimize the sale results on a guaranteed basis.

Using similar approaches, at your death you can minimize or actually recover any investment losses you have suffered in your lifetime. Simply buy a policy to the extent of your loss and your heirs will recover what they would have received at your death. Since you have enough to live on, the loss might be considered temporary during your lifetime and magically it reappears on your statement at your death. It is psychologically satisfying and should produce great peace of mind.

You may have to buy only half as much insurance because of the tax savings you can realize. If you buy the full amount of the loss it may make up for the time factors involved and the cost of money. This is truly wealth preservation and wealth creation.

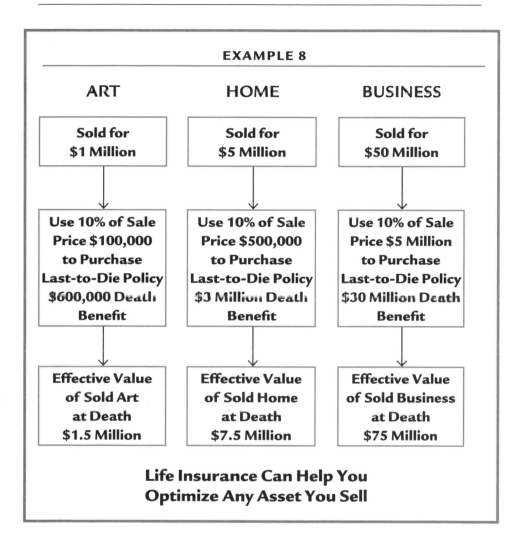

EXAMPLE 8

ART	HOME	BUSINESS
Sold for $1 Million	Sold for $5 Million	Sold for $50 Million
Use 10% of Sale Price $100,000 to Purchase Last-to-Die Policy $600,000 Death Benefit	Use 10% of Sale Price $500,000 to Purchase Last-to-Die Policy $3 Million Death Benefit	Use 10% of Sale Price $5 Million to Purchase Last-to-Die Policy $30 Million Death Benefit
Effective Value of Sold Art at Death $1.5 Million	Effective Value of Sold Home at Death $7.5 Million	Effective Value of Sold Business at Death $75 Million

Life Insurance Can Help You Optimize Any Asset You Sell

CHAPTER 8

Increase Your IRA Up to 50 Times

The epitome of all wealth creation and preservation is demonstrated in this concept. There is a major loss for your heirs at your death, since the IRA receives no step-up in basis and they must pay both income and estate taxes, which could cost as much as 70%. There is wealth creation since I will optimize this net asset many, many times. Recover your 70% tax loss and more.

If you have a $1 million IRA, after all taxes at your death[s] your heirs will receive approximately $300,000. The right path to follow is to take a $1 million distribution after age 59½ while you are alive and pay the income tax. The remaining approximately $650,000 is now used to buy a life expectancy last-to-die survivorship policy on you and your spouse for approximately $15 million. This is up to a 50-fold increase over the $300,000 you would have received, if you qualify. Why would anyone advise you differently? More important, why would you follow such advice?

These figures become incredibly large at greater amounts.

You can arrange any part or all of your IRA depending on your own objectives as indicated in example 9 on the following page:

EXAMPLE 9			
IRA Amount	After Estate Tax Net Value At Death	After Income Tax vs. Net Value Before Death	Net Value Before Death Purchases Death Benefit
$500,000	$150,000	$325,000	$8,000,000
$1,000,000	$300,000	$650,000	$15,000,000
$2,000,000	$600,000	$1,300,000	$30,000,000
$5,000,000	$1,500,000	$3,000,000	$68,000,000
$10,000,000	$3,000,000	$6,000,000	$136,000,000

Many tax advisors consider an IRA sacred since it compounds tax free. But I always ask for whom? It may compound tax free but 70% goes to Uncle Sam. What good is it if you do not need the IRA to live on?

Another mistaken and wrong approach for maximization is the extended IRA approach. While this can transfer the IRA to your children, it will still impose an estate tax. The income tax will be deferred until it is distributed. A simple taxable distribution with the proceeds used to purchase a life insurance policy in an irrevocable trust will in most every case substantially do better than any extended IRA.

CHAPTER 9

Create, Maximize and Optimize All Assets— Change Wrong to Right; Small Changes, Big Results

The social security caper. You are age 65. You receive $3,000 monthly social security for a total of $36,000 yearly. You pay approximately $14,000 income tax for a net income of $22,000 yearly. You do not need this money to live on. Give it to charity or your own charitable foundation. There will be no income tax since it will be offset by the charitable deduction of the gift. The charity will have the use of the full $36,000.

The charity uses the $36,000 yearly to purchase a $3.5 million last-to-die survivorship life insurance policy on you and your spouse. If you use my life expectancy approach the $36,000 yearly can buy as much as $10 million.

It really isn't a difficult decision to make if you don't need your social security to live on; $22,000 a year for you or up to $10 million for charity, which ultimately will produce, at 5% interest, up to $500,000 a year to be given away. (See example 10 on the following page.)

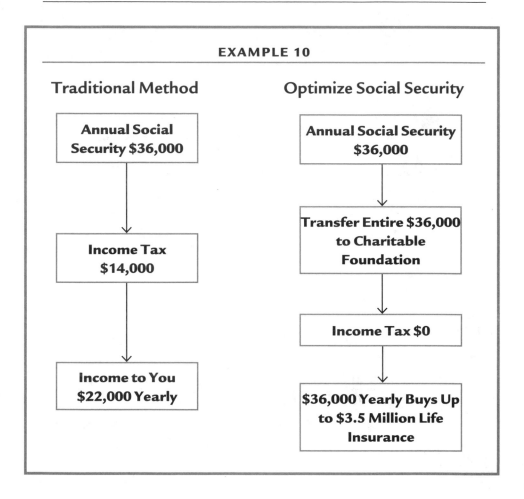

EXAMPLE 10

Traditional Method

Optimize Social Security

Annual Social Security $36,000

Annual Social Security $36,000

Income Tax $14,000

Transfer Entire $36,000 to Charitable Foundation

Income Tax $0

Income to You $22,000 Yearly

$36,000 Yearly Buys Up to $3.5 Million Life Insurance

The perpetual lottery or structured settlement. You have just won a $20 million lottery or a structured settlement. It could be royalties or any major financial windfall. There is an IRS code section known as "income in respect of a decedent" that calls for estate taxes to be levied on the current value of future income. The IRS figures the present value of all future income at the owner's death and charges estate taxes accordingly. If you don't plan for this tax it can have a financially devastating effect on your family at your death. Any tremendous win can cause a forced liquidation and a financial mess.

Let's assume you won $20 million in a lottery. It is paid to you at the rate of $1 million a year over a 20-year period. If you live over the entire 20 years and spend the money, estate taxes may not be a problem. But if you die before the payment term is over, the remainder of the payments due will become part of the estate and taxes will be due. Where will you get the money to pay the taxes? In all probability the family will have to borrow the tax money against the future lottery income, greatly devaluing it.

You buy a last-to-die survivorship policy on you and your spouse for the approximately $10 million tax that would be due at the beginning. The premium would be about $100,000 a year. You should be receiving about $1 million a year from the lottery, so you would be allocating only 10% for this approach.

If you don't die before the end of the payout period and your heirs don't need the insurance for estate taxes, the remainder of the insurance can be used like a second lottery win. This time the win will be for the heirs as they recapture the portion of the prize their parents spent. Ten million dollars at 10% will produce an effective second lottery win in perpetuity.

This same approach can be used for a structured settlement or any windfall. Everyone dies richer. (See example 11 on the following page.)

45

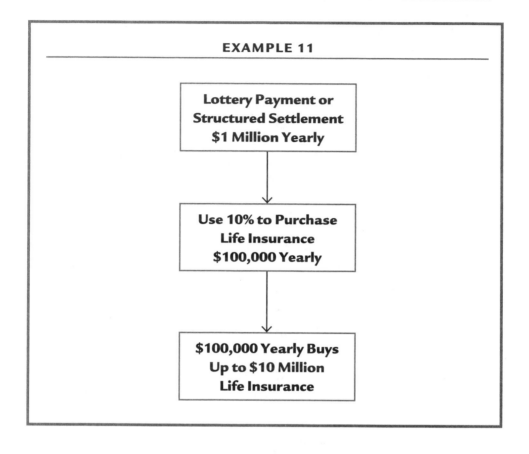

EXAMPLE 11

Lottery Payment or
Structured Settlement
$1 Million Yearly

Use 10% to Purchase
Life Insurance
$100,000 Yearly

$100,000 Yearly Buys
Up to $10 Million
Life Insurance

Triple the value of your home for your heirs. Your home is worth $1 million. You borrow $100,000 through a home equity loan. The yearly interest is 7%, or $7,000. You purchase a $2.5 million last-to-die survivorship life expectancy policy on you and your spouse for a single payment of $100,000. When you both die your heirs will receive the $1 million home less the $100,000 loan plus the $2.5 million policy, for a total of $3.4 million versus the original $1 million home. You have effectively more than tripled the value of your home at a cost of $7,000 a year. Where else can you invest $7,000 a year, tax deductible, and create an extra $2.5 million?

If you have a more expensive home of $2 million or more you may want to borrow $1 million and buy the same type of policy. The $1 million would purchase approximately $25 million. This will produce at your deaths the same $2 million home less the $1 million loan plus the $25 million death benefit for a total of $26 million versus the original $2 million. This is a 13-fold increase and the cost was only approximately $70,000 yearly interest, which could possibly be made tax deductible. (See example 12 on the following page.)

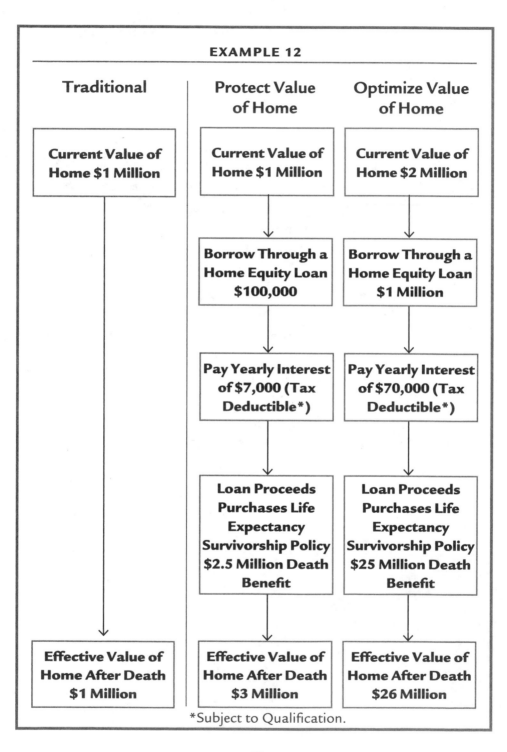

EXAMPLE 12

Traditional	Protect Value of Home	Optimize Value of Home
Current Value of Home $1 Million	Current Value of Home $1 Million	Current Value of Home $2 Million
	↓	↓
	Borrow Through a Home Equity Loan $100,000	Borrow Through a Home Equity Loan $1 Million
	↓	↓
	Pay Yearly Interest of $7,000 (Tax Deductible*)	Pay Yearly Interest of $70,000 (Tax Deductible*)
	↓	↓
	Loan Proceeds Purchases Life Expectancy Survivorship Policy $2.5 Million Death Benefit	Loan Proceeds Purchases Life Expectancy Survivorship Policy $25 Million Death Benefit
↓	↓	↓
Effective Value of Home After Death $1 Million	Effective Value of Home After Death $3 Million	Effective Value of Home After Death $26 Million

*Subject to Qualification.

Convert your debts to assets. You are worth $10 million. You have debt of $1 million. You would like to know that at your deaths your heirs will not have the responsibility of paying back the $1 million debt. Arrange another loan for $500,000, bringing your total loan up to $1.5 million. Gift the $500,000 to an irrevocable trust. The trust purchases a one-payment last-to-die survivorship insurance policy for $5 million. At death $5 million is available to your heirs tax free. This pays off your original $1 million debt plus the new $500,000 debt for a total of $1.5 million. There is still $3.5 million left. You have effectively turned your $1 million debt into a $3.5 million asset. (See example 13 on the following page.)

EXAMPLE 13

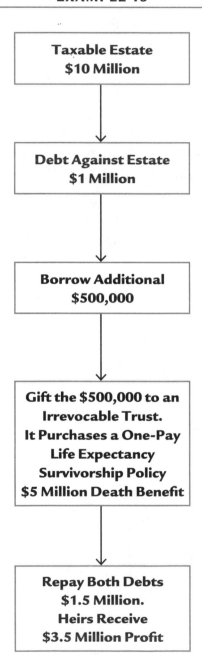

Taxable Estate
$10 Million

Debt Against Estate
$1 Million

Borrow Additional
$500,000

Gift the $500,000 to an
Irrevocable Trust.
It Purchases a One-Pay
Life Expectancy
Survivorship Policy
$5 Million Death Benefit

Repay Both Debts
$1.5 Million.
Heirs Receive
$3.5 Million Profit

Wrong way: Pay off your debt.

Right way: Turn your debt into an asset.

Recover taxes previously paid. This program is similar to turning debts into assets. Choose any amount of income or capital gains taxes you would like to recover. You may have made a major gain on a particular investment and paid taxes of $2 million. Borrow $200,000 at approximately 7% interest of $14,000 yearly. Transfer the $200,000 to an irrevocable trust. The trust purchases a $2.2 million last-to-die survivorship policy with the $200,000. At the deaths of you and your spouse your heirs receive $2.2 million tax free. This recovers the taxes you had paid as well as the $200,000 life insurance premiums.

You can adjust this up or down in accordance with your tax loss and own objectives. Obviously a $5 million tax loss would require $500,000 to recover the taxes and premiums.

(See example 14 on the following page.)

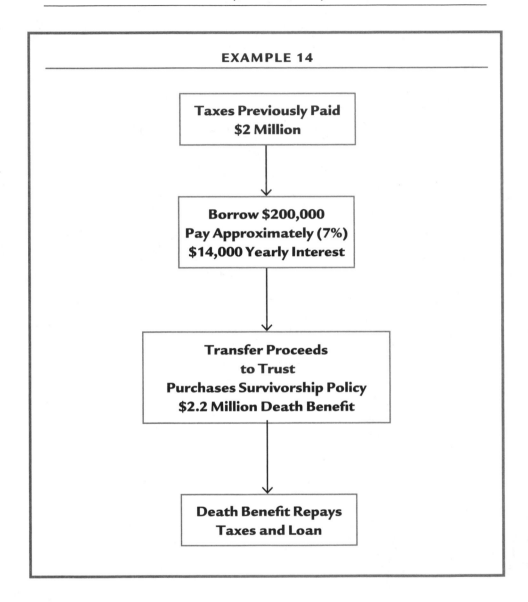

EXAMPLE 14

Taxes Previously Paid
$2 Million

Borrow $200,000
Pay Approximately (7%)
$14,000 Yearly Interest

Transfer Proceeds
to Trust
Purchases Survivorship Policy
$2.2 Million Death Benefit

Death Benefit Repays
Taxes and Loan

Wrong way: Do nothing; suffer the tax loss for your family.
Right way: Recover every tax dollar paid and more.

Don't lose any art. You have collected art for a lifetime. It is now worth more than $5 million. You have always insured your collection for its full value. No collector would ever go without insurance. Yet, at your death, half of the value of your collection will be decimated by estate taxes. You either give it away to a museum to avoid taxes or effectively lose half of the value of your art in taxes. Why wouldn't you buy the type of insurance that would protect this from happening? Why would you feel one type of insurance is right and the other is wrong? Moreover, buying life insurance can even recover the cost of the premiums as well as the taxes. Simply spend 10% more premium; buy 10% more insurance and all expenses will be covered.

You can remove one painting from the wall, sell it and use the proceeds to purchase the insurance to protect the rest of the collection. You could also use the collection as collateral and borrow the necessary premium. This technique will cost you only interest each year, which will be less than the annual premium. (See example 15 on the following page.)

EXAMPLE 15

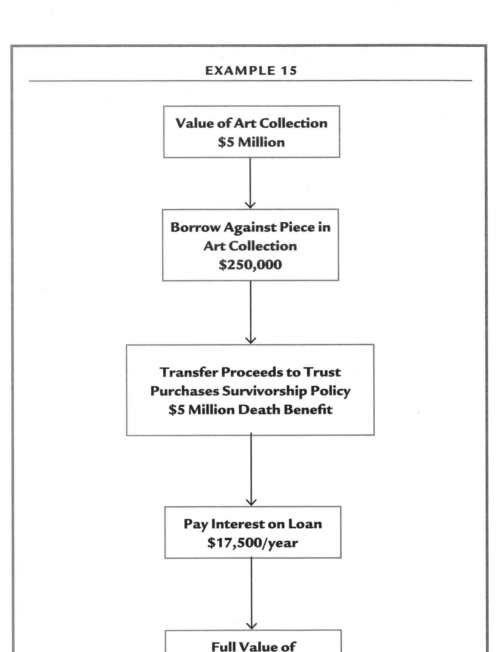

There is no reason for such trauma when the answer is so simple.

Wrong way: Lose your art. Buy only one type of insurance.
Right way: Keep your art. Buy the right insurance.

Guarantee your stock portfolio. You have $3 million of stock. This is money for your heirs and charities, since you have more than enough money to live on without it. You want to make sure the entire principal is there at your deaths no matter what happens to the market.

Simply take 10%, $300,000 from your margin account. It will probably cost you about $21,000 yearly interest, which you do not have to pay, since you can accrue it. The $300,000 can be used to buy a one-payment last-to-die survivorship policy on you and your spouse for about $3 million. This will not only guarantee any loss but it could provide a substantial additional profit at your deaths.

(See example 16 on the following page.)

EXAMPLE 16

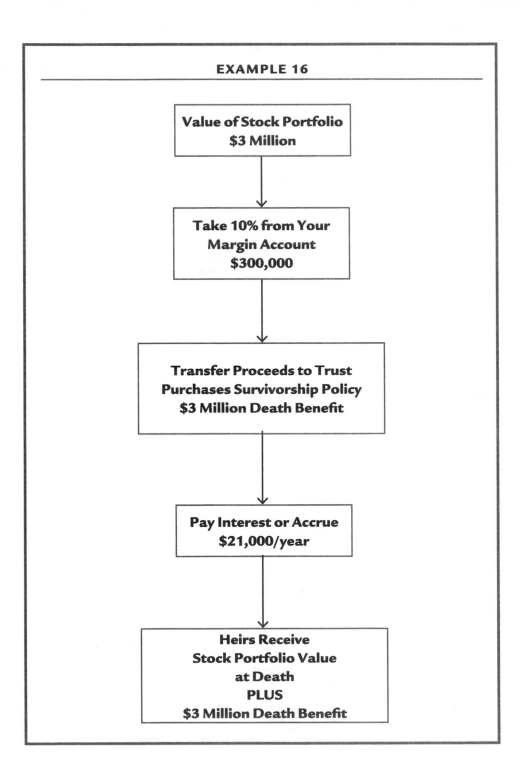

If you are fortunate enough not to lose any money in the market and make substantial profit, then the same insurance can be used to offset the additional estate taxes that will have to be paid on those gains. Either way, you have guaranteed your stock portfolio.

Wrong way: Leave your portfolio subject to loss.
Right way: Guarantee no loss.

Increase your CD and Muni bond yields up to 15%. You have $5 million of bonds. You make 5% for a yearly total of $250,000. You purchase an immediate annuity, depending on your age, which can return up to 15% for a total of $750,000 yearly. This approach provides a better return because it is based on principal and interest. This means there is nothing left for your heirs at your death. You wish to leave them the same $5 million you would have if you had retained your bonds, or at least the $2.5 million they would have received after estate taxes.

Keep 66% of your 15% income, approximately $500,000. This effectively doubles your original 5%. Take the remaining 5%, or $250,000, and buy an insurance policy on your life for about $5 million. At your death, your heirs will receive the original $5 million back and you will have enjoyed a doubled 10% yearly return during your lifetime. If structured properly, it is possible you will have doubled the net return for your heirs as well as yourself.

(See example 17 on the following page.)

EXAMPLE 17

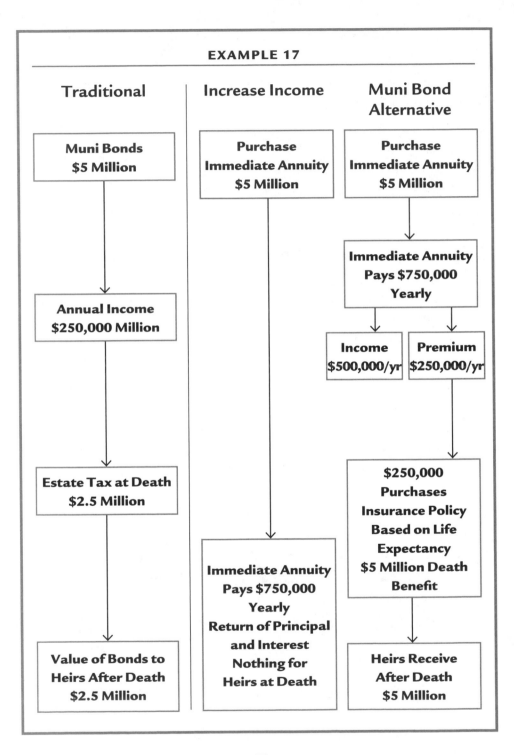

Traditional	Increase Income	Muni Bond Alternative
Muni Bonds $5 Million	**Purchase Immediate Annuity $5 Million**	**Purchase Immediate Annuity $5 Million**
Annual Income $250,000 Million		**Immediate Annuity Pays $750,000 Yearly**
		Income $500,000/yr — **Premium $250,000/yr**
Estate Tax at Death $2.5 Million		**$250,000 Purchases Insurance Policy Based on Life Expectancy $5 Million Death Benefit**
Value of Bonds to Heirs After Death $2.5 Million	**Immediate Annuity Pays $750,000 Yearly Return of Principal and Interest Nothing for Heirs at Death**	**Heirs Receive After Death $5 Million**

Wrong way: Continue 5%, $250,000 return yearly and leave heirs $2.5 million.

Right way: Double return to 10%, $500,000 return yearly and leave heirs up to $5 million.

Increase yearly $12,000 gifts to $3 million for your heirs. The IRS allows you to give $12,000 a year to as many people as you wish, gift tax free. You can give this to your children, grandchildren and others; your spouse can do the same.

If your heirs don't need the money at this time or you wish to leave them a greater sum at your deaths, transfer the $12,000 yearly to each person you choose and have them buy a life expectancy last-to-die survivorship policy on you and your spouse for approximately $3 million. In this manner for each $12,000 you gift each year, you will remove $12,000 from your estate and save about $6,000 in estate taxes. Furthermore, you will create $3 million tax free. In other words, at a net cost of $6,000 yearly you are really removing from your estate $3 million without taxes.

(See example 18 on the following page.)

If you enjoy doing numbers this means you and your spouse together can give away tax free $6 million to your heirs at a net cost of $12,000 yearly. There is no other way to accomplish these results. Now do one more final exercise. If you can afford it and you qualify, with 3 children and 7 grandchildren you have 10 entities. You may transfer $240,000 yearly at a net cost of $120,000. This will create at your deaths $48 million without estate taxes, legally.

EXAMPLE 18

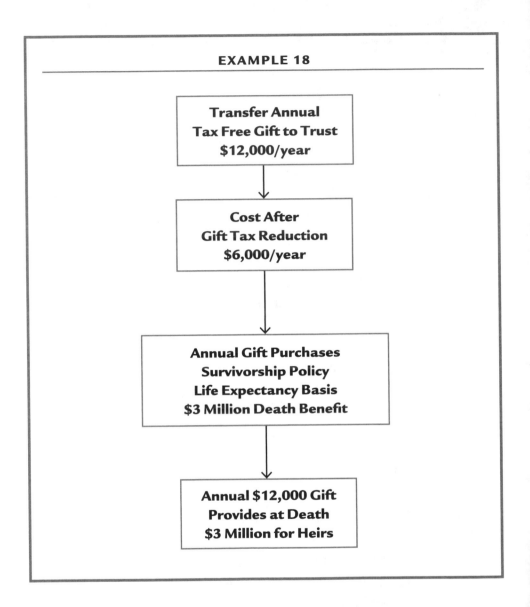

Wrong way: Give conventional $12,000 gifts.
Right way: Maximize $12,000 gifts. Eliminate estate taxes.

Avoid forced liquidation and wasted liquidity. If you do not have liquid assets available at your death to pay your estate taxes, it could be very costly. Forced liquidation could be at fire sale prices for your heirs. This will make the taxes even more onerous and create a higher percentage of your assets to be paid. (See example 19 below.)

Being liquid at your death in anticipation of the taxes to be paid can be very costly. You lose the opportunity of using that money for more productive returns.

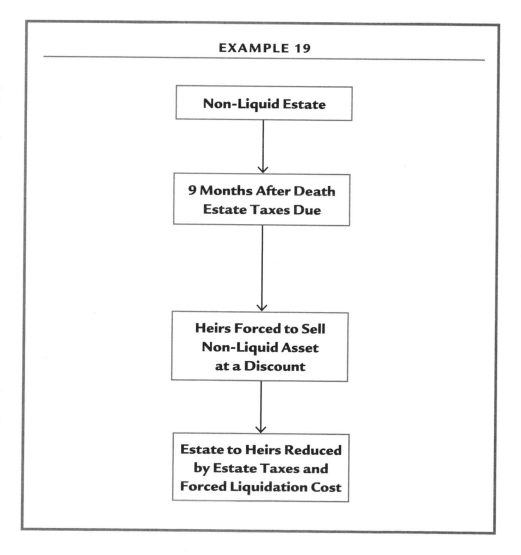

EXAMPLE 19

Non-Liquid Estate

9 Months After Death
Estate Taxes Due

Heirs Forced to Sell
Non-Liquid Asset
at a Discount

Estate to Heirs Reduced
by Estate Taxes and
Forced Liquidation Cost

Wrong way: Stay liquid.

Right way: Buy insurance to create liquidity.

All insurance premiums become tax deductible at death. Remember, insurance premiums and even gift taxes that you pay remove those assets from your estate. Effectively at your death those assets would be worth only half. Therefore, insurance premiums and taxes cost you only half, or you could say they were effectively tax deductible and Uncle Sam paid half of the costs.

CHAPTER 10

The Revolutionary Secondary Market: Life Insurance Grows Up and Becomes a True Asset

I was always amazed that there was no secondary market in life insurance. You could sell your art, collectables, real estate, stock, bonds, jewelry, cars, etc. But there was no market for your life insurance policy, even though it was an asset. You could only surrender your policy back to the company for its cash value, which could amount to pennies on the dollar. It always seemed to me that a market value representing the present value of the death benefit should exist. This was the beginning of lifetime settlements.

Finally, in the last 7 years, this has come to be. You can now sell a policy based on your age and current health for many times your cash value in most cases. This has created a new market for life insurance and added great value to your policy. This is truly a hidden asset that now can be taken advantage of.

If you no longer need a policy for tax purposes, or you do not want to leave a policy to a particular heir, or you no longer wish to pay the premiums, you may sell your policy in the senior settlement market. If the offer exceeds the cash value you may wish to sell it rather than surrender it.

You may also wish to improve your current policy, lower the premium or increase the death benefit by using the proceeds from the sale. You may also want to give a larger policy to charity using the same asset.

If you paid over the years a lot less than you received upon the sale of your policy, you may make a substantial profit. Even if you were not concerned with a profit, you might simply recover all or a part of the premiums you paid.

Over the past few years, billions of dollars of insurance have been bought and are being sold. Depending on the age and the health of the insureds, sellers of the policies are receiving 10% to 20% and more of the death benefit. Much of this money is being used to purchase more efficient policies. Over the years to come, more and more cash from these proceeds will be available for this purpose and this should produce huge amounts of new insurance policies. These can be used to pay estate taxes and optimize assets for heirs and favorite charities as well as to create new larger assets. There may be outstanding profits for you personally using this technique as an investment alternative in your portfolio.

(See example 20 opposite.)

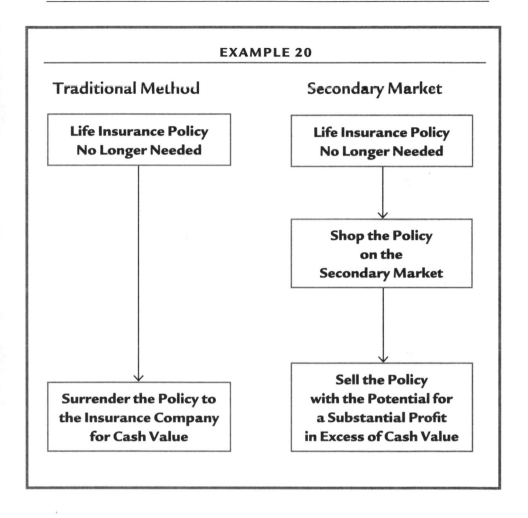

EXAMPLE 20

Traditional Method	Secondary Market
Life Insurance Policy No Longer Needed	**Life Insurance Policy No Longer Needed**
	Shop the Policy on the Secondary Market
Surrender the Policy to the Insurance Company for Cash Value	**Sell the Policy with the Potential for a Substantial Profit in Excess of Cash Value**

CHAPTER 11

Live Rich and Die Rich— Insurance Pays Off In Life or Death

All policies come with options after the first two years. If you died during that period your beneficiaries would have received the death proceeds. If you wish to continue the policy you would continue to pay the premiums. If you borrowed the original money against your stock and bond portfolio or real estate to buy the policy, you could pay back the loan or arrange additional loans.

Your third option is to sell the policy in the institutional world. All three of these options are very valuable and have added to the asset value of your policy.

The following are some of the policy sales I have been involved with.

MALE AGE 75   **$9 MILLION DEATH BENEFIT**

Cost Basis	$ 315,000
Sale Price	$1,290,000
PROFIT	**$ 975,000**

FEMALE AGE 73 **$20 MILLION DEATH BENEFIT**

    Cost Basis $1,500,000

    <u>Sale Price $3,050,000</u>

    PROFIT   **$1,550,000**

MALE AGE 77 **$7.5 MILLION DEATH BENEFIT**

    Cost Basis $ 550,000

    <u>Sale Price $2,400,000</u>

    PROFIT   **$1,850,000**

MALE AGE 77 **$5 MILLION DEATH BENEFIT**

    Cost Basis $ 440,000

    <u>Sale Price $1,850,000</u>

    PROFIT   **$1,410,000**

MALE AGE 79 **$10 MILLION DEATH BENEFIT**

    Cost Basis $ 505,044

    <u>Sale Price $1,300,000</u>

    PROFIT   **$ 794,956**

MALE AGE 79 **$15 MILLION DEATH BENEFIT**

    Cost Basis $ 956,000

    <u>Sale Price $5,175,000</u>

    PROFIT   **$4,219,000**

MALE AGE 78 **$5 MILLION DEATH BENEFIT**

    Cost Basis $ 440,263

    <u>Sale Price $1,850,000</u>

    PROFIT   **$1,409,737**

FEMALE AGE 82   **$5 MILLION DEATH BENEFIT**

Cost Basis	$ 294,000
Sale Price	$ 600,000
PROFIT	**$ 306,000**

MALE AGE 81   **$10 MILLION DEATH BENEFIT**

Cost Basis	$ 540,000
Sale Price	$1,057,000
PROFIT	**$ 517,000**

MALE AGE 86   **$32.2 MILLION DEATH BENEFIT**

Cost Basis	$2,991,022
Sale Price	$9,000,000
PROFIT	**$6,008,978**

FEMALE AGE 77   **$13 MILLION DEATH BENEFIT**

Cost Basis	$1,451,263
Sale Price	$1,700,000
PROFIT	**$ 248,737**

FEMALE AGE 81   **$3.4 MILLION DEATH BENEFIT**

Cost Basis	$ 119,000
Sale Price	$ 731,000
PROFIT	**$ 612,000**

MALE AGE 78   **$27.8 MILLION DEATH BENEFIT**

Cost Basis	$2,167,628
Sale Price	$7,872,000
PROFIT	**$5,704,372**

MALE / FEMALE AGE 79
$6 MILLION DEATH BENEFIT

Cost Basis	$ 96,000
Sale Price	$1,520,000
PROFIT	**$1,424,000**

MALE AGE 74 $4.5 MILLION DEATH BENEFIT

Cost Basis	$ 795,270
Sale Price	$1,180,000
PROFIT	**$ 384,730**

FEMALE AGE 86 $10 MILLION DEATH BENEFIT

Cost Basis	$1,200,000
Sale Price	$4,250,000
PROFIT	**$3,050,000**

MALE AGE 82 $7 MILLION DEATH BENEFIT

Cost Basis	$1,040,000
Sale Price	$1,640,000
PROFIT	**$ 600,000**

These policies have produced incredible returns. As long as these markets continue, the demand should remain high and the insurance industry will be an excellent source of investment alternatives. Policies are being re-priced to accommodate the over-estimated lapse ratio that had been anticipated. Most policies are being purchased by institutions and funds specializing in this area rather than individuals. They see this providing as good, if not better returns than stock portfolios. As long as the policies economically and mathematically produce the proper results, there is no reason for the market not to continue. Furthermore, this not only provides outstanding returns but excellent diversification. It is a win-win situation for all. Most important, this has been a consumer victory. It adds extra value to the insurance policy as an asset and provides another excellent reason for the public to purchase insurance with another backup exit in case of any emergency. It certainly will bring new value to the insurance sales representatives all over the world who bring and explain this product to their customers.

There are many in the industry who feel selling of insurance after two years is wrong. It is important that you choose insurance companies that will accept this concept. Does the end justify the means? Once a policy has been purchased and it is completely thought out at the end of two years, why wouldn't the customer keep the policy? If it is good for an investor to buy it, it must be better for the client to keep it. My client created a $20 million death benefit at a cost of $250,000 a year. What alternative program can you purchase in that manner at the age of 74 with a life expectancy of 12 years to create that much money? Even if she lives 20 years to 94, she still will have paid only $5 million to create $20 million with certain interesting tax ramifications. You have taken $5 million out of an estate that would be worth $2.5 million after taxes and you have created $20 million, if structured properly, tax free. Anyone with substantial assets of $5 million, $10 million, $20 million, $30 million to $100 million should easily be convinced that a policy should be continued in order to pay estate taxes as one option on a pay-as-you-go plan or to create huge money for children and charity using the above figures. On the other hand, if the client wants to sell the policy and he qualifies, the option is available.

The secondary market, as it continues to grow, will become known as one of the most important developments in the history of life insurance. It will certainly be credited as one of the greatest incentives ever created for the sale of this incredible product. Eventually even the industry itself will recognize this added value.

CHAPTER 12

Are You Paying Too Much for Your Insurance?

Insurance is a continually evolving product. Even though you may be older, if you have retained your health, you may find you can still reduce your premium or increase the death benefit for the same outlay.

You will find you can reduce your cost by using the surrender value from your current policy or the superior proceeds from the policy being sold in the secondary market, if you qualify.

Simply call your insurance man and make an application for a new policy with the appropriate medical examination. If he were doing his job properly, he would have called you already. You will find many options available if you receive an excellent health rating. A new company, a new approach, a new policy may improve everything. At least, give it a chance.

(See example 21 on the following page.)

EXAMPLE 21

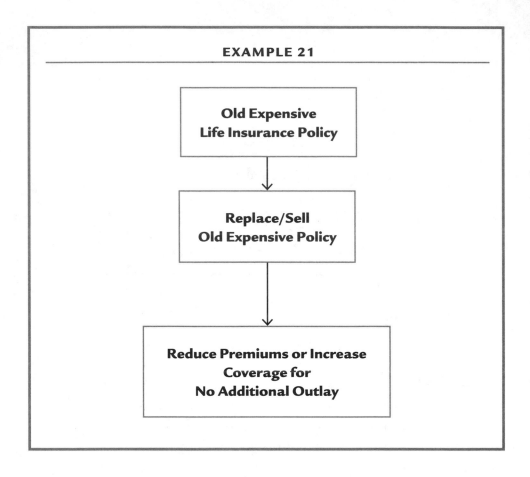

Wrong way: Do nothing. Join the other ostriches.
Right way: Open your mind. Try anything.

CHAPTER 13

Charity:
Give Until It Feels Good

Life insurance and charity go hand in hand. You can give substantial sums at a great guaranteed discount using a policy. When you leave your assets to charity, your real estate or stocks can be up or down. Your heirs can question the contributions in the courts. When you give an insurance policy, it is a gift at inception and will never change and cannot be contested by your heirs. Besides removing the assets from your estate you will also receive a tax deduction when you buy and donate the policy.

You can gift old existing policies you no longer need. You can purchase new policies. You can even give substantial policies at no cost and actually make a profit, based on the tax deduction.

How can you give money to charity at no cost and actually make a profit? Say you buy a policy if you are over 70. Hold it for two years, and then sell the policy in the secondary market. Recover the original premium and donate the profit that you realize to charity. Since you have recovered your outlay, the donation cost you nothing, yet it is still tax deductible, which will make you a profit to the extent of your tax savings. The charity then buys a life expectancy last-to-die survivorship policy on you and your spouse and receives a greatly enhanced gift at your deaths.

These are the actual numbers. You are approximately age 70. You buy a policy for about $10 million at a total cost of $250,000 for two years. You sell the policy after two years for at least 15% of the death benefit, approximately $1,500,000. You recover your own $250,000 and donate to charity the balance of your profit of approximately $1,000,000 after taxes. The charity purchases a life expectancy last-to-die survivorship policy on you and your spouse for a death benefit of approximately $25,000,000 if you qualify. The cost to you is nothing since you have recovered your original outlay. You actually make a profit since your charitable contribution of $1,000,000 is deductible and should create about $400,000 tax savings. Ultimately upon your deaths the charity could receive up to $25,000,000.

If you choose, the charity could be your own charitable foundation. In this manner you will create a substantial family foundation and your children could even be trustees. They would also receive the allowable trustee fees. Everyone wins: you, your insurance company, your insurance agent, your favorite charities, your children and the institution that bought your policy.

(See example 22 on facing page.)

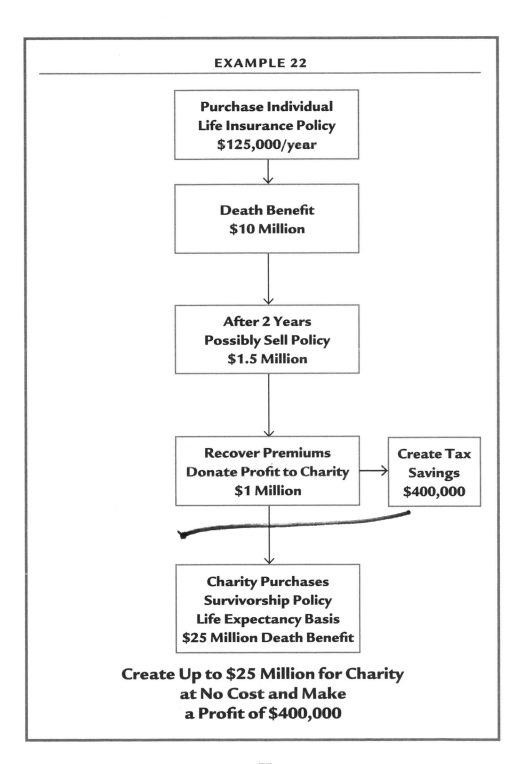

EXAMPLE 22

**Purchase Individual
Life Insurance Policy
$125,000/year**

**Death Benefit
$10 Million**

**After 2 Years
Possibly Sell Policy
$1.5 Million**

**Recover Premiums
Donate Profit to Charity
$1 Million**

**Create Tax
Savings
$400,000**

**Charity Purchases
Survivorship Policy
Life Expectancy Basis
$25 Million Death Benefit**

**Create Up to $25 Million for Charity
at No Cost and Make
a Profit of $400,000**

CHAPTER 14

Important Facts and Caveats About This Book

There are many points that must be understood in order to read this book and get the most out of it. I often refer to last-to-die survivorship policies. These are policies on two people, usually husband and wife. Sometimes these policies can include an ex-spouse or any two family members. If one of the two members is not insurable a surrogate insured can be used. Any concept described for two people can be used with one individual, if more applicable.

All information in this book is based on 2006 tax law. You should consult with your tax professional relative to any changes. References to eliminating estate taxes are effectively accomplished by offsetting the cost of any estate tax paid with the death benefit proceeds from life insurance.

I constantly refer to a life expectancy policy. This is a new concept I developed over the past years to lower the premiums and resulting cost of any policy. It is a funding technique. You purchase the same regular policy you would regularly buy but instead of funding it to last past 100 or until death, the same policy is funded to or past your life expectancy, which is usually 85 depending on your current age or ages. This substantially reduces the premium. The less you pay the shorter period the insurance covers you. The more you pay the longer period you are covered. You can continue your policy at any time by simply paying an additional premium to make up for the lesser premium paid. However, in this manner you don't overpay since your premiums are based on your life expectancy. If you live longer you pay at a later date larger premiums. Why pay extra premiums to an insurance company when you don't really know how long you are going to live? The more money you don't pay, the more money you have to invest, the more you will compound and accumulate in case you outlive your expectancy. In this manner you pay as you go for the time you need. This is very cost efficient since there are never any medical or qualification requirements necessary after the original purchase.

In order to really understand the huge savings accomplished by using the life expectancy funding approach, I have included Rate Tables for various ages using life expectancies for male, female and last-to-die policies at ages 85, 90, 95, 100 and beyond on a preferred basis.

There are also guaranteed policies. In the past you would purchase a policy based on current assumptions of interest, expense and mortality. Obviously, this was less expensive. You can now buy policies for very little more that are completely guaranteed for the period you choose and can also be extended.

I also refer to borrowing. Many people do not like to put their own money into insurance. Since most people I work with are over 65 years and worth between $5 million and $400 million, they usually have no mortgage against their homes or margin against their stocks. It is very easy for them to borrow against these assets and use none of their own cash flow in purchasing insurance. There is only the minimal yearly interest, which can even be accrued. Since life insurance doesn't go up or down, there is really very little risk in using this leverage.

All figures and examples of premiums I have used throughout the book are based on individuals from ages 60 to 70 and are only estimates. The charts on the following pages will give you a better approximate example based upon your own age.

Rate Charts

As I have done with all my books, I am including here a set of charts and tables that will give you rates based on a preferred rating at your age. More important, you will find charts that will help you customize these amazing concepts to your own financial and estate situation. If you require additional information or more exact rates, you may call my office at 1-800-DIE-RICH (800-343-7424) for a personalized, no obligation and confidential proposal. However, if you prefer, you can consult the following pages to determine an estimate based on your health and marital status.

Remember that these estimates are not actual quotations. They are actual quotes from different companies based on one-pay and life-time rates, but there are too many variables that affect insurance costs to include them all here. However, there is rarely any reason for you to pay more than the lowest prices from the highest rated insurance companies, since all companies pay the same at death.

Many of the policies are based on guaranteed rates. In other cases, they are based on current assumptions of mortality, interest and expenses. I have further broken down the charts to include male, female and last-to-die survivorship polices. They are all based on $1 million so you can prorate up or down. There may be additional discounts above certain amounts. There are 3-4 companies listed under each category of one-pay and annual premium.

Remember, any of these rates can change at any time before you actually buy a policy and these charts are based on generalizations and averages. From all of this information you now may be able to customize your understanding of how a concept and a policy will work for you. Good luck with your own, *'you buy, you die, it pays'* concepts, but always remember there is no substitute for a real live insurance man or woman.

Past Age 100, To Age 100, To Age 95, To Age 90 and To Age 85

MALE AGE 30

One Payment for $1,000,000 of Death Benefit

Insurance Company	Past Age 100	To Age 100	To Age 95	To Age 90	To Age 85
Company A	$87,941*	$86,313*	$74,362	$58,265	$48,128
Company B	$91,233*	$71,951	$64,199	$54,433	$44,611
Company C	$73,759*	$68,302*	$63,307*	$56,637*	$49,524*
Company D	$65,644	$65,644	$61,745	$56,324	$50,142

Annual Payment for $1,000,000 of Death Benefit

Insurance Company	Past Age 100	To Age 100	To Age 95	To Age 90	To Age 85
Company A[1]	$3,638*	$3,545*	$3,115*	$2,641*	$2,059*
Company B	$4,833*	$3,405	$3,053	$2,611	$2,169
Company C	$3,969*	$3,684*	$3,426*	$3,084*	$2,724*
Company D	$3,775	$3,775	$3,555	$3,254	$2,916

* Guaranteed for the period illustrated.

Those not marked are based on current assumptions and have varying guarantee lengths.

Illustrations assume an individual of the above-stated health with a preferred rating.

Some products may contain a blend of term life insurance to reduce premiums.

[1] First year is a $25,000 Required Annual Premium and premiums shown above are from year two to end of term.

Past Age 100, To Age 100, To Age 95, To Age 90 and To Age 85

MALE AGE 35

One Payment for $1,000,000 of Death Benefit

Insurance Company	Past Age 100	To Age 100	To Age 95	To Age 90	To Age 85
Company A	$105,285*	$103,257*	$93,014	$71,856	$58,566
Company B	$108,034*	$94,782	$84,910	$71,906	$58,909
Company C	$90,009*	$82,895*	$76,399*	$67,724*	$58,474*
Company D	$83,357	$83,357	$78,148	$70,902	$62,640

Annual Payment for $1,000,000 of Death Benefit

Insurance Company	Past Age 100	To Age 100	To Age 95	To Age 90	To Age 85
Company A[1]	$4,708*	$4,591*	$4,062*	$3,485*	$2,775*
Company B	$5,840*	$4,596	$4,141	$3,544	$2,954
Company C	$4,936*	$4,546*	$4,208*	$3,761*	$3,291*
Company D	$4,874	$4,874	$4,576	$4,172	$3,718

*Guaranteed for the period illustrated.

Those not marked are based on current assumptions and have varying guarantee lengths.

Illustrations assume an individual of the above-stated health with a preferred rating.

Some products may contain a blend of term life insurance to reduce premiums.

[1]First year is a $25,000 Required Annual Premium and premiums shown above are from year two to end of term.

Past Age 100, To Age 100, To Age 95, To Age 90 and To Age 85

MALE AGE 40

One Payment for $1,000,000 of Death Benefit

Insurance Company	Past Age 100	To Age 100	To Age 95	To Age 90	To Age 85
Company A	$123,215*	$120,822*	$109,346*	$89,213	$71,801
Company B	$128,817*	$111,716	$99,212	$83,153	$66,815
Company C	$109,637*	$100,378*	$91,923*	$80,634*	$68,594*
Company D	$128,164*	$110,117	$101,755	$90,393	$77,472

Annual Payment for $1,000,000 of Death Benefit

Insurance Company	Past Age 100	To Age 100	To Age 95	To Age 90	To Age 85
Company A[1]	$5,948*	$5,808*	$5,171*	$4,481*	$3,623*
Company B	$7,038*	$5,541	$4,958	$4,215	$3,466
Company C	$6,118*	$5,625*	$5,181*	$4,594*	$3,979*
Company D	$6,823*	$5,929	$5,504	$4,932	$4,290

*Guaranteed for the period illustrated

Those not marked are based on current assumptions and have varying guarantee lengths.
Illustrations assume an individual of the above-stated health with a preferred rating.
Some products may contain a blend of term life insurance to reduce premiums.
[1]First year is a $25,000 Required Annual Premium and premiums shown above are from year two to end of term.

Past Age 100, To Age 100, To Age 95, To Age 90 and To Age 85

MALE AGE 45

One Payment for $1,000,000 of Death Benefit

Insurance Company	Past Age 100	To Age 100	To Age 95	To Age 90	To Age 85
Company A	$143,959*	$141,080*	$127,284*	$109,948	$87,080
Company B	$156,031*	$144,777	$128,845	$107,406	$85,706
Company C	$134,637*	$122,561*	$111,533*	$96,808*	$81,105*
Company D	$151,889*	$138,351	$127,480	$112,708	$95,709

Annual Payment for $1,000,000 of Death Benefit

Insurance Company	Past Age 100	To Age 100	To Age 95	To Age 90	To Age 85
Company A[1]	$7,587*	$7,410*	$6,605*	$5,741*	$4,658*
Company B	$8,613*	$7,454	$6,694	$5,681	$4,670
Company C	$7,711*	$7,059*	$6,473*	$5,701*	$4,895*
Company D	$8,390*	$7,683	$7,123	$6,373	$5,533

*Guaranteed for the period illustrated.

Those not marked are based on current assumptions and have varying guarantee lengths.

Illustrations assume an individual of the above-stated health with a preferred rating.

Some products may contain a blend of term life insurance to reduce premiums.

[1]First year is a $25,000 Required Annual Premium and premiums shown above are from year two to end of term.

EXAMPLE CHARTS

Past Age 100, To Age 100, To Age 95, To Age 90 and To Age 85

MALE AGE 50

One Payment for $1,000,000 of Death Benefit

Insurance Company	Past Age 100	To Age 100	To Age 95	To Age 90	To Age 85
Company A	$162,561*	$159,986*	$145,754*	$125,302*	$101,955*
Company B	$179,403*	$168,410	$147,933	$121,095	$93,555
Company C	$167,455*	$151,690*	$137,295*	$118,073*	$97,574*
Company D	$179,956*	$170,803	$156,610	$137,325	$114,907

Annual Payment for $1,000,000 of Death Benefit

Insurance Company	Past Age 100	To Age 100	To Age 95	To Age 90	To Age 85
Company A[1]	$8,988*	$8,845*	$8,124*	$7,312*	$6,147*
Company B	$10,239*	$8,975	$7,984	$6,698	$5,391
Company C	$9,914*	$9,049*	$8,276*	$7,259*	$6,203*
Company D	$10,364*	$9,869	$9,129	$8,139	$7,038

* Guaranteed for the period illustrated.
Those not marked are based on current assumptions and have varying guarantee lengths.
Illustrations assume an individual of the above-stated health with a preferred rating.
Some products may contain a blend of term life insurance to reduce premiums.
[1] First year is a $25,000 Required Annual Premium and premiums shown above are from year two to end of term.

Past Age 100, To Age 100, To Age 95, To Age 90 and To Age 85

MALE AGE 55

One Payment for $1,000,000 of Death Benefit

Insurance Company	Past Age 100	To Age 100	To Age 95	To Age 90	To Age 85
Company A	$194,792*	$191,175*	$170,947*	$143,922*	$118,100*
Company B	$209,205*	$192,826*	$179,833*	$148,546	$113,537
Company C	$208,717*	$186,065*	$167,206*	$142,024*	$115,169*
Company D	$208,815*	$206,660	$187,948	$162,524	$132,493

Annual Payment for $1,000,000 of Death Benefit

Insurance Company	Past Age 100	To Age 100	To Age 95	To Age 90	To Age 85
Company A[1]	$11,576*	$11,386*	$10,588*	$9,563*	$8,015*
Company B	$12,314*	$11,935	$10,596	$8,778	$7,091
Company C	$12,763*	$11,607*	$10,581*	$9,236*	$7,848*
Company D	$12,575*	$12,515	$11,525	$10,206	$8,741

*Guaranteed for the period illustrated.
Those not marked are based on current assumptions and have varying guarantee lengths.
Illustrations assume an individual of the above-stated health with a preferred rating.
Some products may contain a blend of term life insurance to reduce premiums.
[1]First year is a $25,000 Required Annual Premium and premiums shown above are from year two to end of term.

Past Age 100, To Age 100, To Age 95, To Age 90 and To Age 85

MALE AGE 60

One Payment for $1,000,000 of Death Benefit

Insurance Company	Past Age 100	To Age 100	To Age 95	To Age 90	To Age 85
Company A	$237,300*	$232,709*	$205,973*	$174,516*	$141,405*
Company B	$240,480*	$220,962*	$205,466*	$166,569	$125,844
Company C	$252,305*	$225,064*	$200,188*	$166,973*	$131,631*
Company D	$253,256*	$252,197	$227,491	$193,171	$153,080

Annual Payment for $1,000,000 of Death Benefit

Insurance Company	Past Age 100	To Age 100	To Age 95	To Age 90	To Age 85
Company A[1]	$15,560*	$15,308*	$14,415*	$13,174*	$11,183*
Company B	$14,431*	$14,376*	$12,797	$10,640	$8,695
Company C	$16,413*	$14,853*	$13,478*	$11,682*	$9,848*
Company D	$16,156*	$16,194	$14,865	$13,103	$11,163

*Guaranteed for the period illustrated.

Those not marked are based on current assumptions and have varying guarantee lengths.

Illustrations assume an individual of the above-stated health with a preferred rating.

Some products may contain a blend of term life insurance to reduce premiums.

[1]First year is a $25,000 Required Annual Premium and premiums shown above are from year two to end of term.

Past Age 100, To Age 100, To Age 95, To Age 90 and To Age 85

MALE AGE 65

One Payment for $1,000,000 of Death Benefit

Insurance Company	Past Age 100	To Age 100	To Age 95	To Age 90	To Age 85
Company A	$289,260*	$279,765*	$238,357*	$197,385*	$137,173
Company B	$297,302*	$297,302*	$251,326*	$202,076	$145,910
Company C	$313,453*	$276,856*	$243,437*	$198,911*	$152,952*
Company D	$309,516*	$297,804	$263,725	$216,274	$162,564

Annual Payment for $1,000,000 of Death Benefit

Insurance Company	Past Age 100	To Age 100	To Age 95	To Age 90	To Age 85
Company A[1]	$20,905*	$20,420*	$18,530*	$15,135	$11,167
Company B	$19,005*	$18,998*	$17,251	$14,412	$11,642
Company C	$21,685*	$19,552*	$17,695*	$15,295*	$13,002*
Company D	$21,269*	$20,489	$18,671	$16,270	$13,595

*Guaranteed for the period illustrated.

Those not marked are based on current assumptions and have varying guarantee lengths. Illustrations assume an individual of the above-stated health with a preferred rating.

Some products may contain a blend of term life insurance to reduce premiums.

[1]First year is a $25,000 Required Annual Premium for Past 100, To Age 100 and To Age 95. The Required Annual Premium To Age 90 and To Age 85 is $16,036. Premiums shown above are from year two to end of term.

EXAMPLE CHARTS

Past Age 100, To Age 100, To Age 95, To Age 90 and To Age 85

MALE AGE 70

One Payment for $1,000,000 of Death Benefit

Insurance Company	Past Age 100	To Age 100	To Age 95	To Age 90	To Age 85
Company A	$345,659*	$333,828*	$282,418*	$216,022	$141,826
Company B	$360,658*	$328,977*	$308,449	$233,235	$159,522
Company C	$389,201*	$339,632*	$294,371*	$235,834*	$171,978*
Company D	$376,655*	$353,516	$306,185	$242,132	$170,924

Annual Payment for $1,000,000 of Death Benefit

Insurance Company	Past Age 100	To Age 100	To Age 95	To Age 90	To Age 85
Company A[1]	$28,276*	$27,784*	$24,108	$18,800	$13,795
Company B	$25,039*	$25,039*	$23,529	$19,526	$15,822
Company C	$29,150*	$26,222*	$23,727*	$20,702*	$17,690*
Company D	$28,208*	$26,893	$24,413	$21,167	$17,533

*Guaranteed for the period illustrated.

Those not marked are based on current assumptions and have varying guarantee lengths. Illustrations assume an individual of the above-stated health with a preferred rating. Some products may contain a blend of term life insurance to reduce premiums.

[1] First year Required Annual Premium of $20,916 for To Age 90 and To Age 85. Premiums shown above are from year two to end of term. To Age 95, 100 and Past 100 are the level premium shown.

Past Age 100, To Age 100, To Age 95, To Age 90 and To Age 85

MALE AGE 75

One Payment for $1,000,000 of Death Benefit

Insurance Company	Past Age 100	To Age 100	To Age 95	To Age 90	To Age 85
Company A	$418,142*	$399,679*	$320,578*	$218,394	$125,689
Company B	$444,631*	$400,646*	$362,286	$256,230	$157,057
Company C	$461,505*	$392,282*	$329,105*	$243,557*	$162,521*
Company D	$427,341	$427,341	$345,061	$253,583	$157,887

Annual Payment for $1,000,000 of Death Benefit

Insurance Company	Past Age 100	To Age 100	To Age 95	To Age 90	To Age 85
Company A[1]	$38,109*	$36,894*	$29,339	$23,205	$16,694
Company B	$34,547*	$34,547*	$32,508	$26,569	$21,760
Company C	$37,896*	$33,759*	$30,308*	$25,822*	$24,236*
Company D	$39,022*	$38,267	$32,400	$26,602	$20,985

*Guaranteed for the period illustrated.

Those not marked are based on current assumptions and have varying guarantee lengths.

Illustrations assume an individual of the above-stated health with a preferred rating.

Some products may contain a blend of term life insurance to reduce premiums.

[1]First year Required Annual Premium of $23,926 for To Age 90 and To Age 85. Premiums shown above are from year two to end of term. To Age 95, 100 and Past 100 are the level premium shown.

Past Age 100, To Age 100, To Age 95, To Age 90 and To Age 85

MALE AGE 80

One Payment for $1,000,000 of Death Benefit

Insurance Company	Past Age 100	To Age 100	To Age 95	To Age 90	To Age 85
Company A	$568,280*	$539,228*	$413,405*	$275,405*	$98,478*
Company B	$552,770*	$491,862*	$375,919	$237,433	$86,913
Company C	$477,111	$477,111	$343,609	$221,795	$103,826
Company D	$646,405*	$533,540	$419,914	$262,059	$102,867

Annual Payment for $1,000,000 of Death Benefit

Insurance Company	Past Age 100	To Age 100	To Age 95	To Age 90	To Age 85
Company A[1]	$62,302*	$59,686*	$49,682*	$40,099*	$17,122*
Company B	$50,261*	$50,261*	$41,283	$33,843	$23,628
Company C	$48,296	$48,296	$38,008	$30,400	$23,702
Company D[2]	$69,153*	$57,737	$48,916	$36,241	$18,988

*Guaranteed for the period illustrated.

Those not marked are based on current assumptions and have varying guarantee lengths.
Illustrations assume an individual of the above-stated health with a preferred rating.
Some products may contain a blend of term life insurance to reduce premiums.

[1] First year Required Annual Premium of $55,996 for To Age 90 and To Age 85. Premiums shown above are from year two to end of term. To Age 95, 100 and Past 100 are the level premium shown.

[2] First year Required Annual Premium of $52,734 for To Age 95, To Age 90 and To Age 85. Premiums shown above are from year two to end of term. To Age 100 and Past Age 100 are the level premium shown.

Past Age 100, To Age 100, To Age 95, To Age 90 and To Age 85

MALE AGE 85

One Payment for $1,000,000 of Death Benefit

Insurance Company	Past Age 100	To Age 100	To Age 95	To Age 90	To Age 85
Company A	$672,555*	$582,000*	$400,554	$166,470	N/A
Company B	$568,016	$568,016	$372,302	$182,055	N/A
Company C	$766,474*	$567,456	$399,444	$163,759	

Annual Payment for $1,000,000 of Death Benefit

Insurance Company	Past Age 100	To Age 100	To Age 95	To Age 90	To Age 85
Company A	$79,590*	$79,590*	$62,110	$46,449	N/A
Company B	$71,670	$71,670	$55,284	$42,766	N/A
Company C [1]	$108,243*	$70,078	$54,929	$22,414	N/A

*Guaranteed for the period illustrated.

Those not marked are based on current assumptions and have varying guarantee lengths.

Illustrations assume an individual of the above-stated health with a preferred rating.

Some products may contain a blend of term life insurance to reduce premiums.

[1] First year Required Annual Premium of $106,164 for To Age 100, To Age 95, To Age 90. Premiums shown above are from year two to end of term. Past Age 100 are the level premium shown.

Past Age 100, To Age 100, To Age 95, To Age 90 and To Age 85

FEMALE AGE 30

One Payment for $1,000,000 of Death Benefit

Insurance Company	Past Age 100	To Age 100	To Age 95	To Age 90	To Age 85
Company A	$78,216*	$66,931	$52,339	$42,989	$35,553
Company B	$70,763*	$57,067	$48,818	$40,643	$33,138
Company C	$76,144*	$52,930	$47,537	$41,119	$34,472
Company D	$52,126	$52,126	$47,404	$41,788	$36,196

Annual Payment for $1,000,000 of Death Benefit

Insurance Company	Past Age 100	To Age 100	To Age 95	To Age 90	To Age 85
Company A[1]	$2,937*	$2,794*	$2,175*	$1,621*	$1,052
Company B	$3,705*	$2,675	$2,302	$1,936	$1,602
Company C	$3,578*	$2,686	$2,419	$2,102	$1,782
Company D	$2,967	$2,967	$2,703	$2,394	$2,090

*Guaranteed for the period illustrated.

Those not marked are based on current assumptions and have varying guarantee lengths.
Illustrations assume an individual of the above-stated health with a preferred rating.
Some products may contain a blend of term life insurance to reduce premiums.
[1]First year is a $25,000 Required Annual Premium and premiums shown above are from year two to end of term.

EXAMPLE CHARTS

Past Age 100, To Age 100, To Age 95, To Age 90 and To Age 85

FEMALE AGE 35

One Payment for $1,000,000 of Death Benefit

Insurance Company	Past Age 100	To Age 100	To Age 95	To Age 90	To Age 85
Company A	$94,141*	$84,501	$65,369	$53,119	$43,377
Company B	$85,039*	$71,711	$61,361	$51,075	$41,787
Company C	$90,511*	$65,686	$58,672	$50,324	$41,652
Company D	$75,893*	$65,510*	$58,822*	$51,963*	$45,372*

Annual Payment for $1,000,000 of Death Benefit

Insurance Company	Past Age 100	To Age 100	To Age 95	To Age 90	To Age 85
Company A[1]	$3,935*	$3,757*	$2,979*	$2,278*	$1,562*
Company B	$4,533*	$3,427	$2,955	$2,492	$2,079
Company C	$4,441*	$3,386	$3,037	$2,622	$2,205
Company D	$4,094*	$3,553*	$3,210*	$2,864*	$2,539*

*Guaranteed for the period illustrated.

Those not marked are based on current assumptions and have varying guarantee lengths. Illustrations assume an individual of the above-stated health with a preferred rating.

Some products may contain a blend of term life insurance to reduce premiums.

[1]First year is a $25,000 Required Annual Premium and premiums shown above are from year two to end of term.

Past Age 100, To Age 100, To Age 95, To Age 90 and To Age 85

FEMALE AGE 40

One Payment for $1,000,000 of Death Benefit

Insurance Company	Past Age 100	To Age 100	To Age 95	To Age 90	To Age 85
Company A	$106,076*	$103,629*	$81,977	$65,958	$53,217
Company B	$103,999*	$83,701	$70,789	$58,203	$46,756
Company C	$108,619*	$82,849	$73,751	$62,924	$51,629
Company D	$92,660*	$79,166*	$70,475*	$61,562*	$52,998*

Annual Payment for $1,000,000 of Death Benefit

Insurance Company	Past Age 100	To Age 100	To Age 95	To Age 90	To Age 85
Company A¹	$4,682*	$4,542*	$3,829*	$3,114*	$2,358*
Company B	$5,578*	$4,078	$3,485	$2,915	$2,403
Company C	$5,500*	$4,362	$3,905	$3,365	$2,822
Company D	$5,085*	$4,375*	$3,926*	$3,475*	$3,054*

* Guaranteed for the period illustrated.
Those not marked are based on current assumptions and have varying guarantee lengths.
Illustrations assume an individual of the above-stated health with a preferred rating.
Some products may contain a blend of term life insurance to reduce premiums.
¹First year is a $25,000 Required Annual Premium and premiums shown above are from year two to end of term.

EXAMPLE CHARTS

Past Age 100, To Age 100, To Age 95, To Age 90 and To Age 85

FEMALE AGE 45

One Payment for $1,000,000 of Death Benefit

Insurance Company	Past Age 100	To Age 100	To Age 95	To Age 90	To Age 85
Company A	$119,925*	$117,115*	$101,876	$80,856	$64,148
Company B	$128,579*	$109,412	$92,450	$75,351	$59,788
Company C	$128,852*	$103,737	$91,927	$77,782	$62,956
Company D	$112,733*	$95,193*	$83,896*	$72,310*	$61,178*

Annual Payment for $1,000,000 of Death Benefit

Insurance Company	Past Age 100	To Age 100	To Age 95	To Age 90	To Age 85
Company A[1]	$5,801*	$5,631*	$4,781*	$3,917*	$2,992*
Company B	$6,898*	$5,503	$4,710	$3,924	$3,219
Company C	$6,748*	$5,604	$5,005	$4,298	$3,590
Company D	$6,324*	$5,391*	$4,802*	$4,213*	$3,664*

*Guaranteed for the period illustrated.
Those not marked are based on current assumptions and have varying guarantee lengths.
Illustrations assume an individual of the above-stated health with a preferred rating.
Some products may contain a blend of term life insurance to reduce premiums.
[1]First year is a $25,000 Required Annual Premium and premiums shown above are from year two to end of term.

Past Age 100, To Age 100, To Age 95, To Age 90 and To Age 85

FEMALE AGE 50

One Payment for $1,000,000 of Death Benefit

Insurance Company	Past Age 100	To Age 100	To Age 95	To Age 90	To Age 85
Company A	$137,078*	$134,067*	$116,817*	$93,589*	$74,152*
Company B	$148,102*	$127,191	$105,844	$84,751	$65,499
Company C	$148,251*	$126,551	$111,122	$92,419	$73,050
Company D	$139,701*	$116,845*	$102,125*	$87,027*	$72,521*

Annual Payment for $1,000,000 of Death Benefit

Insurance Company	Past Age 100	To Age 100	To Age 95	To Age 90	To Age 85
Company A[1]	$7,104*	$6,932*	$6,021*	$5,068*	$3,940*
Company B	$8,259*	$6,599	$5,588	$4,609	$3,729
Company C	$8,426*	$7,051	$6,261	$5,328	$4,393
Company D	$8,053*	$6,820*	$6,047*	$5,299*	$4,567*

*Guaranteed for the period illustrated.

Those not marked are based on current assumptions and have varying guarantee lengths.

Illustrations assume an individual of the above-stated health with a preferred rating.

Some products may contain a blend of term life insurance to reduce premiums.

[1]First year is a $25,000 Required Annual Premium and premiums shown above are from year two to end of term.

Past Age 100, To Age 100, To Age 95, To Age 90 and To Age 85

FEMALE AGE 55

One Payment for $1,000,000 of Death Benefit

Insurance Company	Past Age 100	To Age 100	To Age 95	To Age 90	To Age 85
Company A	$162,436*	$158,273*	$134,319*	$104,422*	$83,932*
Company B	$172,385*	$158,967	$130,339	$101,251	$76,338
Company C	$175,729*	$155,013	$134,830	$109,975	$84,640
Company D	$171,948*	$142,032*	$122,764*	$103,002*	$84,016*

Annual Payment for $1,000,000 of Death Benefit

Insurance Company	Past Age 100	To Age 100	To Age 95	To Age 90	To Age 85
Company A[1]	$9,109*	$8,874*	$7,688*	$6,553*	$5,045
Company B	$9,967*	$8,626	$7,233	$5,843	$4,820
Company C	$10,540*	$8,991	$7,945	$6,710	$5,471
Company D	$10,242*	$8,605*	$7,584*	$6,577*	$5,651*

*Guaranteed for the period illustrated.

Those not marked are based on current assumptions and have varying guarantee lengths.

Illustrations assume an individual of the above-stated health with a preferred rating.

Some products may contain a blend of term life insurance to reduce premiums.

[1]First year is a $25,000 Required Annual Premium and premiums shown above are from year two to end of term.

Past Age 100, To Age 100, To Age 95, To Age 90 and To Age 85

FEMALE AGE 60

One Payment for $1,000,000 of Death Benefit

Insurance Company	Past Age 100	To Age 100	To Age 95	To Age 90	To Age 85
Company A	$196,265*	$191,107*	$159,677*	$125,647*	$100,780*
Company B	$200,725*	$182,092	$145,370	$112,223	$82,878
Company C	$217,541*	$192,678	$166,178	$133,171	$99,880
Company D	$210,541*	$171,177*	$145,824*	$119,821*	$95,149*

Annual Payment for $1,000,000 of Death Benefit

Insurance Company	Past Age 100	To Age 100	To Age 95	To Age 90	To Age 85
Company A[1]	$11,992*	$11,685*	$10,357*	$8,979	$6,839
Company B	$11,939*	$10,370	$8,547	$6,970	$5,936
Company C	$13,639*	$11,769	$10,384	$8,755	$7,129
Company D	$13,073*	$10,880*	$9,522*	$8,195*	$7,008*

*Guaranteed for the period illustrated.

Those not marked are based on current assumptions and have varying guarantee lengths. Illustrations assume an individual of the above-stated health with a preferred rating.

Some products may contain a blend of term life insurance to reduce premiums.

[1]First year and second year Required Annual Premium of $7,051 for To Age 85. Premiums shown above are from year three to end of term. First year Required Annual Premium of $25,000 for To Age 90, 95, 100 and Past 100. Premiums shown above are from year two to end of term.

EXAMPLE CHARTS

Past Age 100, To Age 100, To Age 95, To Age 90 and To Age 85

FEMALE AGE 65

One Payment for $1,000,000 of Death Benefit

Insurance Company	Past Age 100	To Age 100	To Age 95	To Age 90	To Age 85
Company A	$237,072*	$223,453*	$172,796*	$131,078	$89,133
Company B	$248,724*	$224,343	$179,558	$133,450	$94,591
Company C	$257,771*	$227,280	$190,680	$146,802	$102,612
Company D	$255,656*	$203,167*	$169,360*	$135,508*	$103,351*

Annual Payment for $1,000,000 of Death Benefit

Insurance Company	Past Age 100	To Age 100	To Age 95	To Age 90	To Age 85
Company A[1]	$15,919*	$15,048*	$12,031*	$9,268	$6,762
Company B	$15,550*	$13,738	$11,474	$9,199	$7,377
Company C	$17,027*	$14,745	$12,866	$10,648	$8,331
Company D	$16,706*	$13,720*	$11,886*	$10,168*	$8,817*

*Guaranteed for the period illustrated.

Those not marked are based on current assumptions and have varying guarantee lengths. Illustrations assume an individual of the above-stated health with a preferred rating. Some products may contain a blend of term life insurance to reduce premiums.

[1]First year and second year Required Annual Premium of $10,421 for To Age 85. Premiums shown above are from year three to end of term. First year Required Annual Premium of $25,000 for To Age 90, 95, 100 and Past 100. Premiums shown above are from year two to end of term.

Past Age 100, To Age 100, To Age 95, To Age 90 and To Age 85

FEMALE AGE 70

One Payment for $1,000,000 of Death Benefit

Insurance Company	Past Age 100	To Age 100	To Age 95	To Age 90	To Age 85
Company A	$286,473*	$268,989	$209,500	$143,000	$92,200
Company B	$300,625*	$283,169	$213,539	$152,015	$101,251
Company C	$310,285*	$240,020*	$195,446*	$153,109*	$109,587*

Annual Payment for $1,000,000 of Death Benefit

Insurance Company	Past Age 100	To Age 100	To Age 95	To Age 90	To Age 85
Company A[1]	$21,504*	$21,428*	$15,886	$11,936	$8,706
Company B	$19,818*	$19,205	$15,373	$12,212	$9,786
Company C	$21,639*	$17,550*	$15,119*	$13,078*	$11,092*

*Guaranteed for the period illustrated.

Those not marked are based on current assumptions and have varying guarantee lengths. Illustrations assume an individual of the above-stated health with a preferred rating.

Some products may contain a blend of term life insurance to reduce premiums.

[1] First year Required Annual Premium of $13,274 for To Age 90 and To Age 85. First year Required Annual Premium of $25,000 for Past 100. Premiums shown above are from year two to end of term. To Age 100 and To Age 95 are the level premiums shown.

Past Age 100, To Age 100, To Age 95, To Age 90 and To Age 85

FEMALE AGE 75

One Payment for $1,000,000 of Death Benefit

Insurance Company	Past Age 100	To Age 100	To Age 95	To Age 90	To Age 85
Company A	$349,676*	$326,888*	$229,371	$153,994	$82,607
Company B	$363,417*	$323,573*	$244,303	$159,542	$90,308
Company C	$376,680*	$281,568*	$227,384*	$166,209*	$102,545*

Annual Payment for $1,000,000 of Death Benefit

Insurance Company	Past Age 100	To Age 100	To Age 95	To Age 90	To Age 85
Company A[1]	$29,768*	$25,385	$20,237	$15,802	$10,660
Company B	$26,043*	$25,522	$20,360	$15,734	$12,190
Company C	$28,617*	$22,959*	$20,174*	$17,221*	$14,270*

*Guaranteed for the period illustrated.

Those not marked are based on current assumptions and have varying guarantee lengths. Illustrations assume an individual of the above-stated health with a preferred rating.

Some products may contain a blend of term life insurance to reduce premiums.

[1]First year Required Annual Premium of $16,004 for To Age 90 and To Age 85. Premiums shown above are from year two to end of term. Past Age 100, To Age 100 and To Age 95 are the level premiums shown.

Past Age 100, To Age 100, To Age 95, To Age 90 and To Age 85

FEMALE AGE 80

One Payment for $1,000,000 of Death Benefit

Insurance Company	Past Age 100	To Age 100	To Age 95	To Age 90	To Age 85
Company A	$442,797*	$381,944	$268,511	$158,239	$61,172
Company B	$450,453*	$325,873*	$247,331	$154,107*	$74,166*
Company C	$558,869*	$451,621	$335,314	$193,826	$74,043

Annual Payment for $1,000,000 of Death Benefit

Insurance Company	Past Age 100	To Age 100	To Age 95	To Age 90	To Age 85
Company A	$38,860*	$34,158	$27,670	$21,798	$17,175
Company B	$40,612*	$40,612	$30,146	$24,360	$19,638
Company C	$38,365*	$30,849*	$26,755*	$21,928*	$20,287*

* Guaranteed for the period illustrated.

Those not marked are based on current assumptions and have vary ng guarantee lengths.

Illustrations assume an individual of the above-stated health with a preferred rating.

Some products may contain a blend of term life insurance to reduce premiums.

Past Age 100, To Age 100, To Age 95, To Age 90 and To Age 85

FEMALE AGE 85

One Payment for $1,000,000 of Death Benefit

Insurance Company	Past Age 100	To Age 100	To Age 95	To Age 90	To Age 85
Company A	$592,140*	$463,692	$291,564	$109,374	N/A
Company B	$623,243*	$464,799*	$330,360*	$177,999*	N/A
Company C	$770,602*	$475,665	$297,829	$115,978	N/A

Annual Payment for $1,000,000 of Death Benefit

Insurance Company	Past Age 100	To Age 100	To Age 95	To Age 90	To Age 85
Company A	$64,270*	$53,185	$42,426	$29,919	N/A
Company B	$65,436*	$55,942*	$49,981*	$49,688*	N/A
Company C[1]	$97,788*	$56,015	$40,217	$17,971	N/A

*Guaranteed for the period illustrated.

Those not marked are based on current assumptions and have varying guarantee lengths. Illustrations assume an individual of the above-stated health with a preferred rating. Some products may contain a blend of term life insurance to reduce premiums.

[1] First year is a $68,784 Required Annual Premium for To Age 95 and To Age 90. Premiums shown above are from year two to end of term. Past Age 100 and To Age 100 are the level premiums shown.

Past Age 100, To Age 100, To Age 95, To Age 90 and To Age 85

LAST-TO-DIE MALE AGE 30 / FEMALE AGE 30

One Payment for $1,000,000 of Death Benefit

Insurance Company	Past Age 100	To Age 100	To Age 95	To Age 90	To Age 85
Company A	$46,998*	$43,586*	$30,263*	$20,619*	$12,846*
Company B	$42,062*	$33,880	$28,260	$21,639	$15,251
Company C	$59,643*	$24,417	$18,093	$13,231	$9,837

Annual Payment for $1,000,000 of Death Benefit

Insurance Company	Past Age 100	To Age 100	To Age 95	To Age 90	To Age 85
Company A	$2,181*	$2,035*	$1,471*	$1,012*	$803*
Company B	$1,907*	$1,610	$1,347	$1,040	$705
Company C[1]	$2,623*	$1,092	$781	$541	$501

*Guaranteed for the period illustrated.

Those not marked are based on current assumptions and have varying guarantee lengths.

Illustrations assume an individual of the above-stated health with a preferred rating.

Some products may contain a blend of term life insurance to reduce premiums.

[1]First year is a $2,704 Required Annual Premium for To Age 100, To Age 95, To Age 90, To Age 85. Premiums shown above are from year two to end of term. Past Age 100 are the level premiums shown.

Past Age 100, To Age 100, To Age 95, To Age 90 and To Age 85

LAST-TO-DIE MALE AGE 35 / FEMALE AGE 35

One Payment for $1,000,000 of Death Benefit

Insurance Company	Past Age 100	To Age 100	To Age 95	To Age 90	To Age 85
Company A	$60,508*	$56,089*	$38,710*	$26,058*	$15,873*
Company B	$69,463*	$31,317	$22,840	$16,260	$11,647
Company C	$42,809	$42,809	$31,700	$22,965	$17,292
Company D	$57,359*	$43,821	$36,707	$28,222	$20,152

Annual Payment for $1,000,000 of Death Benefit

Company A	$2,852*	$2,658*	$1,914*	$1,306*	$998*
Company B	$2,650*	$2,112	$1,777	$1,386	$1,017
Company C[1]	$3,120*	$1,455	$1,034	$706	$610

*Guaranteed for the period illustrated.

Those not marked are based on current assumptions and have varying guarantee lengths.

Illustrations assume an individual of the above-stated health with a preferred rating.

Some products may contain a blend of term life insurance to reduce premiums.

[1]First year is a $2,762 Required Annual Premium for To Age 100, To Age 95, To Age 90 and To Age 85. Premiums shown above are from year two to end of term. Past Age 100 are the level premiums shown.

Past Age 100, To Age 100, To Age 95, To Age 90 and To Age 85

LAST-TO-DIE MALE AGE 40 / FEMALE AGE 40

One Payment for $1,000,000 of Death Benefit

Insurance Company	Past Age 100	To Age 100	To Age 95	To Age 90	To Age 85
Company A	$72,409*	$67,222*	$46,171*	$31,052*	$18,687*
Company B	$83,143*	$40,898	$29,448	$20,449	$14,111
Company C	$55,003	$55,003	$40,039	$28,310	$20,695
Company D	$104,241*	$55,997	$42,563	$31,198	$23,187

Annual Payment for $1,000,000 of Death Benefit

Insurance Company	Past Age 100	To Age 100	To Age 95	To Age 90	To Age 85
Company A	$3,516*	$3,287*	$2,389*	$1,634*	$1,198*
Company B[1]	$3,796*	$1,972	$1,397	$943	$762
Company C	$3,273*	$3,245	$2,373	$1,476	$1,253
Company D[2]	$3,680*	$3,440*	$2,620*	$1,950	$1,145*

*Guaranteed for the period illustrated.

Those not marked are based on current assumptions and have varying guarantee lengths. Illustrations assume an individual of the above-stated health with a preferred rating. Some products may contain a blend of term life insurance to reduce premiums.

[1]First year is a $2,837 Required Annual Premium for To Age 100, To Age 95, To Age 90, To Age 85. Premiums shown above are from year two to end of term. Past Age 100 are the level premiums shown.

[2]Year one through year seven is a $2,010 Required Annual Premium for To Age 90, To Age 85. Premiums shown above are from year eight to end of term. Past Age 100, To Age 100 and To Age 95 are the level premiums shown.

Past Age 100, To Age 100, To Age 95, To Age 90 and To Age 85

LAST-TO-DIE MALE AGE 45 / FEMALE AGE 45

One Payment for $1,000,000 of Death Benefit

Insurance Company	Past Age 100	To Age 100	To Age 95	To Age 90	To Age 85
Company A	$89,114*	$82,728*	$55,987*	$37,406*	$22,058*
Company B	$99,759*	$53,525	$36,240	$25,806	$17,128
Company C	$70,966	$70,966	$50,723	$34,882	$24,675
Company D	$126,190*	$74,602	$56,297	$40,111	$28,426

Annual Payment for $1,000,000 of Death Benefit

Insurance Company	Past Age 100	To Age 100	To Age 95	To Age 90	To Age 85
Company A	$4,438*	$4,155*	$3,035*	$2,075*	$1,572*
Company B[1]	$4,567*	$2,679	$1,893	$1,264	$976
Company C[2]	$4,720*	$4,420*	$3,380*	$2,350	$1,350

*Guaranteed for the period illustrated.

Those not marked are based on current assumptions and have varying guarantee lengths.

Illustrations assume an individual of the above-stated health with a preferred rating.

Some products may contain a blend of term life insurance to reduce premiums.

[1]First year is a $2,937 Required Annual Premium for To Age 100, To Age 95, To Age 90, To Age 85. Premiums shown above are from year two to end of term. Past Age 100 are the level premiums shown.

[2]Year one through year seven is a $2,620 Required Annual Premium for To Age 90 and To Age 85. Premiums shown above are from year eight to end of term. Past Age 100, To Age 100 and To Age 95 are the level premiums shown.

Past Age 100, To Age 100, To Age 95, To Age 90 and To Age 85

LAST-TO-DIE MALE AGE 50 / FEMALE AGE 50

One Payment for $1,000,000 of Death Benefit

Insurance Company	Past Age 100	To Age 100	To Age 95	To Age 90	To Age 85
Company A	$107,366*	$99,523*	$66,296*	$43,783*	$24,885*
Company B	$121,729*	$71,435	$50,318	$33,201	$21,058
Company C	$91,816	$91,816	$64,356	$42,946	$29,305
Company D	$144,095*	$96,770	$72,263	$50,022	$33,864

Annual Payment for $1,000,000 of Death Benefit

Insurance Company	Past Age 100	To Age 100	To Age 95	To Age 90	To Age 85
Company A	$5,573*	$5,215*	$3,795*	$2,570*	$2,299*
Company B	$5,597*	$3,693	$3,073	$3,073	$3,073
Company C	$6,300*	$4,489*	$3,269*	$2,324*	$1,979*
Company D[1]	$5,980*	$5,600*	$4,250*	$2,800	$1,540

*Guaranteed for the period illustrated.

Those not marked are based on current assumptions and have varying guarantee lengths. Illustrations assume an individual of the above-stated health with a preferred rating. Some products may contain a blend of term life insurance to reduce premiums.

[1]Year one through year seven is a $3,420 Required Annual Premium for To Age 90, To Age 85. Premiums shown above are from year eight to end of term. Past Age 100, To Age 100 and To Age 95 are the level premiums shown.

EXAMPLE CHARTS

Past Age 100, To Age 100, To Age 95, To Age 90 and To Age 85

LAST-TO-DIE MALE AGE 55 / FEMALE AGE 55

One Payment for $1,000,000 of Death Benefit

Insurance Company	Past Age 100	To Age 100	To Age 95	To Age 90	To Age 85
Company A	$133,535*	$123,487*	$81,013*	$52,936*	$28,797*
Company B	$151,976*	$94,891	$66,076	$42,303	$25,448
Company C	$118,479	$118,479	$79,649	$52,350	$34,187
Company D	$162,073*	$113,799	$83,736	$57,346	$38,580

Annual Payment for $1,000,000 of Death Benefit

Insurance Company	Past Age 100	To Age 100	To Age 95	To Age 90	To Age 85
Company A	$8,280*	$5,896*	$4,274*	$3,031*	$2,318
Company B[1]	$8,342*	$6,108	$4,600	$3,064	$1,913
Company C[2]	$7,140*	$6,650*	$5,000*	$3,300*	$1,700*

* Guaranteed for the period illustrated.

Those not marked are based on current assumptions and have varying guarantee lengths.

Illustrations assume an individual of the above-stated health with a preferred rating.

Some products may contain a blend of term life insurance to reduce premiums.

[1] Year one through year three is a $4,348 Required Annual Premium for To Age 90, To Age 85. Premiums shown above are from year four to end of term. Past Age 100 and To Age 95 are the level premiums shown.

[2] Year one through year seven is a $4,520 Required Annual Premium for To Age 90, To Age 85. Premiums shown above are from year eight to end of term. Past Age 100 and To Age 95 are the level premiums shown.

Past Age 100, To Age 100, To Age 95, To Age 90 and To Age 85

LAST-TO-DIE MALE AGE 60 / FEMALE AGE 60

One Payment for $1,000,000 of Death Benefit

Insurance Company	Past Age 100	To Age 100	To Age 95	To Age 90	To Age 85
Company A	$160,638*	$147,567*	$95,791*	$61,596*	$31,893*
Company B	$182,689*	$124,736	$85,436	$52,559	$29,520
Company C	$151,996	$151,996	$93,629	$62,231	$38,122
Company D	$218,000*	$140,477	$105,327	$69,813	$42,693

Annual Payment for $1,000,000 of Death Benefit

Insurance Company	Past Age 100	To Age 100	To Age 95	To Age 90	To Age 85
Company A	$10,976*	$7,788*	$5,608*	$3,905*	$2,789
Company B[1]	$10,785*	$8,945	$6,702	$4,219	$2,266
Company C[2]	$9,220*	$8,620*	$6,503*	$3,720	$1,600

*Guaranteed for the period illustrated.

Those not marked are based on current assumptions and have varying guarantee lengths.

Illustrations assume an individual of the above-stated health with a preferred rating.

Some products may contain a blend of term life insurance to reduce premiums.

[1]Year one through year three is a $6,264 Required Annual Premium for To Age 90, To Age 85. Premiums shown above are from year four to end of term. Past Age 100, To Age 100 and To Age 95 are the level premiums shown.

[2]Year one through year seven is a $5,990 Required Annual Premium for To Age 90, To Age 85. Premiums shown above are from year eight to end of term. Past Age 100, To Age 100 and To Age 95 are the level premiums shown.

Past Age 100, To Age 100, To Age 95, To Age 90 and To Age 85

LAST-TO-DIE MALE AGE 65 / FEMALE AGE 65

One Payment for $1,000,000 of Death Benefit

Insurance Company	Past Age 100	To Age 100	To Age 95	To Age 90	To Age 85
Company A	$200,328*	$182,123*	$114,606*	$69,856*	$36,136*
Company B	$223,419*	$161,311	$107,558	$62,420	$32,045
Company C	$194,789	$194,789	$111,562	$71,968	$40,452
Company D	$267,000*	$169,063	$122,325	$75,821	$42,001

Annual Payment for $1,000,000 of Death Benefit

Insurance Company	Past Age 100	To Age 100	To Age 95	To Age 90	To Age 85
Company A[1]	$14,126*	$10,880	$7,994	$4,806	$2,525
Company B	$14,715*	$10,364	$7,403	$5,046	$3,311
Company C	$19,207*	$15,031	$8,844	$5,623	$3,253

*Guaranteed for the period illustrated.

Those not marked are based on current assumptions and have varying guarantee lengths. Illustrations assume an individual of the above-stated health with a preferred rating.

Some products may contain a blend of term life insurance to reduce premiums.

[1]Year one through year three is a $8,171 Required Annual Premium for To Age 90, To Age 85. Premiums shown above are from year four to end of term. Past Age 100, To Age 100 and To Age 95 are the level premiums shown.

Past Age 100, To Age 100, To Age 95, To Age 90 and To Age 85

LAST-TO-DIE MALE AGE 70 / FEMALE AGE 70

One Payment for $1,000,000 of Death Benefit

Insurance Company	Past Age 100	To Age 100	To Age 95	To Age 90	To Age 85
Company A	$269,664*	$184,003	$119,739	$66,072	$34,026
Company B	$246,829*	$246,829	$127,034	$76,925	$37,772
Company C	$327,000	$213,258	$148,527	$82,428	$49,837
Company D	$341,665*	$288,908	$144,451	$73,722	$37,912

Annual Payment for $1,000,000 of Death Benefit

Insurance Company	Past Age 100	To Age 100	To Age 95	To Age 90	To Age 85
Company A	$15,243*	$11,885	$8,278	$5,145	$4,604
Company B	$19,956*	$13,826*	$9,564	$6,309	$3,647
Company C	$19,200*	$13,945	$9,952	$5,556	$4,591
Company D	$22,639*	$19,746	$10,390	$5,889	$3,625

*Guaranteed for the period illustrated.

Those not marked are based on current assumptions and have varying guaranteed lengths.
Illustrations assume an individual of the above-stated health with a preferred rating.
Some products may contain a blend of term life insurance to reduce premiums.

Past Age 100, To Age 100, To Age 95, To Age 90 and To Age 85

LAST-TO-DIE MALE AGE 75 / FEMALE AGE 75

One Payment for $1,000,000 of Death Benefit

Insurance Company	Past Age 100	To Age 100	To Age 95	To Age 90	To Age 85
Company A	$330,335*	$220,280	$132,092	$69,802	$32,195
Company B	$309,727	$309,727	$138,356	$72,716	$35,620
Company C	$418,000*	$266,944	$177,510	$96,848	$59,085
Company D	$406,927*	$348,082	$136,055	$65,433	$39,365

Annual Payment for $1,000,000 of Death Benefit

Insurance Company	Past Age 100	To Age 100	To Age 95	To Age 90	To Age 85
Company A	$20,623*	$15,824	$10,504	$6,683	$5,241
Company B	$27,584*	$18,561*	$11,563	$7,069	$5,168
Company C	$27,200*	$19,453	$13,501	$7,708	$5,258
Company D	$30,829*	$26,085	$11,165	$6,363	$5,244

*Guaranteed for the period illustrated.

Those not marked are based on current assumptions and have varying guaranteed lengths.

Illustrations assume an individual of the above-stated health with a preferred rating.

Some products may contain a blend of term life insurance to reduce premiums.

EXAMPLE CHARTS

Past Age 100, To Age 100, To Age 95, To Age 90 and To Age 85

LAST-TO-DIE MALE AGE 80 / FEMALE AGE 80

One Payment for $1,000,000 of Death Benefit

Insurance Company	Past Age 100	To Age 100	To Age 95	To Age 90	To Age 85
Company A	$392,849*	$243,379	$168,641	$93,933	$44,736
Company B	$427,277*	$243,224	$138,164	$62,692	$28,996
Company C	$382,031	$382,031	$128,549	$64,187	$35,896
Company D	$436,705*	$370,744	$120,863	$64,501	$30,689

Annual Payment for $1,000,000 of Death Benefit

Insurance Company	Past Age 100	To Age 100	To Age 95	To Age 90	To Age 85
Company A	$30,127*	$20,184	$13,513	$8,433	$7,778*
Company B	$33,057	$33,057*	$12,640	$8,200	$7,988
Company C	$40,200*	$31,762	$23,334	$14,804	$7,021
Company D	$37,825*	$31,377	$12,189	$8,768	$8,133

*Guaranteed for the period illustrated.

Those not marked are based on current assumptions and have varying guaranteed lengths.
Illustrations assume an individual of the above-stated health with a preferred rating.
Some products may contain a blend of term life insurance to reduce premiums.

Past Age 100, To Age 100, To Age 95, To Age 90 and To Age 85

LAST-TO-DIE MALE AGE 85 / FEMALE AGE 85

One Payment for $1,000,000 of Death Benefit

Insurance Company	Past Age 100	To Age 100	To Age 95	To Age 90	To Age 85
Company A	$497,198*	$241,179	$145,329	$59,511	N/A
Company B	$564,000*	$319,991	$149,942	$48,906	N/A
Company C	$488,136	$488,136	$133,705	$66,310	N/A
Company D	$467,308*	$429,380	$107,964	$46,077	N/A

Annual Payment for $1,000,000 of Death Benefit

Insurance Company	Past Age 100	To Age 100	To Age 95	To Age 90	To Age 85
Company A	$45,198*	$25,006	$20,058	$16,028	N/A
Company B[1]	$47,352*	$32,911	$17,694	$4,002	N/A
Company C	$50,181	$50,181	$17,354	$14,782	N/A
Company D	$48,522*	$44,182	$15,345	$12,387	N/A

* Guaranteed for the period illustrated.

Those not marked are based on current assumptions and have varying guarantee lengths. Illustrations assume an individual of the above-stated health with a preferred rating. Some products may contain a blend of term life insurance to reduce premiums.

[1] First year is a $38,049 Required Annual Premium for To Age 100, To Age 95, To Age 90. Premiums shown above are from year two to end of term. Past Age 100 are the level premiums shown.

$200,000 PURCHASES TO AGE 85

LAST-TO-DIE CHART

Age	One Pay Premium	Death Benefit	Years Covered*	Coverage Lasts*	Yearly Premium from Ages 85-91	Yearly Premium from Ages 85-101
30	$200,000	$26,970,646	54	To Age 85	$303,493	$581,063
35	$200,000	$21,514,237	49	To Age 85	$258,311	$492,804
40	$200,000	$16,877,159	44	To Age 85	$218,861	$415,695
45	$200,000	$13,353,144	39	To Age 85	$186,293	$352,727
50	$200,000	$10,500,088	34	To Age 85	$161,270	$304,002
55	$200,000	$8,474,103	29	To Age 85	$141,918	$267,334
60	$200,000	$7,178,722	24	To Age 85	$128,736	$244,418
65	$200,000	$6,538,598	19	To Age 85	$120,775	$236,159
70	$200,000	$6,095,709	14	To Age 85	$93,267	$194,362
75	$200,000	$6,399,434	9	To Age 85	$86,745	$198,290
80	$200,000	$2,826,184	11	To Age 90	N/A	$274,247

Numbers valid as of August 31, 2006

*Rates are based on preferred underwriting for both individuals on a last-to-die life insurance policy. Any change in interest, mortality charges or underwriting status will not change premium but will affect death benefit.

121

FEDERAL ESTATE TAX BASED ON THE ECONOMIC GROWTH AND TAX RELIEF RECONCILIATION ACT OF 2001

Assets	2006	2007	2008	2009	2010	2011
$2,000,000	$-	$-	$-	$-	$-	$550,000
$2,500,000	$230,000	$225,000	$225,000	$-	$-	$825,000
$3,000,000	$460,000	$450,000	$450,000	$-	$-	$1,100,000
$3,500,000	$690,000	$675,000	$675,000	$-	$-	$1,375,000
$4,000,000	$920,000	$900,000	$900,000	$225,000	$-	$1,650,000
$4,500,000	$1,150,000	$1,125,000	$1,125,000	$450,000	$-	$1,925,000
$5,000,000	$1,380,000	$1,350,000	$1,350,000	$675,000	$-	$2,200,000
$5,500,000	$1,610,000	$1,575,000	$1,575,000	$900,000	$-	$2,475,000
$6,000,000	$1,840,000	$1,800,000	$1,800,000	$1,125,000	$-	$2,750,000
$6,500,000	$2,070,000	$2,025,000	$2,025,000	$1,350,000	$-	$3,025,000
$7,000,000	$2,300,000	$2,250,000	$2,250,000	$1,575,000	$-	$3,300,000
$7,500,000	$2,530,000	$2,475,000	$2,475,000	$1,800,000	$-	$3,575,000
$8,000,000	$2,760,000	$2,700,000	$2,700,000	$2,025,000	$-	$3,850,000
$8,500,000	$2,990,000	$2,925,000	$2,925,000	$2,250,000	$-	$4,125,000
$9,000,000	$3,220,000	$3,150,000	$3,150,000	$2,475,000	$-	$4,400,000
$9,500,000	$3,450,000	$3,375,000	$3,375,000	$2,700,000	$-	$4,675,000
$10,000,000	$3,680,000	$3,600,000	$3,600,000	$2,925,000	$-	$4,950,000
$11,000,000	$4,140,000	$4,050,000	$4,050,000	$3,375,000	$-	$5,500,000
$12,000,000	$4,600,000	$4,500,000	$4,500,000	$3,825,000	$-	$6,050,000
$13,000,000	$5,060,000	$4,950,000	$4,950,000	$4,275,000	$-	$6,600,000
$14,000,000	$5,520,000	$5,400,000	$5,400,000	$4,725,000	$-	$7,150,000

$15,000,000	$5,980,000	$5,850,000	$5,850,000	$5,175,000	$-	$7,700,000
$16,000,000	$6,440,000	$6,300,000	$6,300,000	$5,625,000	$-	$8,250,000
$17,000,000	$6,900,000	$6,750,000	$6,750,000	$6,075,000	$-	$8,800,000
$18,000,000	$7,360,000	$7,200,000	$7,200,000	$6,525,000	$-	$9,350,000
$19,000,000	$7,820,000	$7,650,000	$7,650,000	$6,975,000	$-	$9,900,000
$20,000,000	$8,280,000	$8,100,000	$8,100,000	$7,425,000	$-	$10,450,000
$25,000,000	$10,580,000	$10,350,000	$10,350,000	$9,675,000	$-	$13,200,000
$30,000,000	$12,880,000	$12,600,000	$12,600,000	$11,925,000	$-	$15,950,000
$35,000,000	$15,180,000	$14,850,000	$14,850,000	$14,175,000	$-	$18,700,000
$40,000,000	$17,480,000	$17,100,000	$17,100,000	$16,425,000	$-	$21,450,000
$45,000,000	$19,780,000	$19,350,000	$19,350,000	$18,675,000	$-	$24,200,000
$50,000,000	$22,080,000	$21,600,000	$21,600,000	$20,925,000	$-	$26,950,000
$60,000,000	$26,680,000	$26,100,000	$26,100,000	$25,425,000	$-	$32,450,000
$70,000,000	$31,280,000	$30,600,000	$30,600,000	$29,925,000	$-	$37,950,000
$80,000,000	$35,880,000	$35,100,000	$35,100,000	$34,425,000	$-	$43,450,000
$90,000,000	$40,480,000	$39,600,000	$39,600,000	$38,925,000	$-	$48,950,000
$100,000,000	$45,080,000	$44,100,000	$44,100,000	$43,425,000	$-	$54,450,000

The Economic Growth and Tax Relief Reconciliation Act of 2001 (EGTRRA 2001), reduces the percentage of tax owed and increases the amount excluded from estate tax over a period of years, through 2009. In 2010, the estate tax is repealed. However, without further Congressional action, the federal estate tax will be reinstated in 2011 at the pre-EGTRRA 2001 tax rate of 55% with an exemption of $1,000,000 per person.

COMMISSIONERS 2001 STANDARD ORDINARY MORTALITY TABLE

MALE AND FEMALE
AGE LAST BIRTHDAY

AGE	MALE	FEMALE	AGE	MALE	FEMALE	AGE	MALE	FEMALE
0	75.67	79.87	45	32.73	36.33	90	3.20	4.64
1	74.73	78.90	46	31.82	35.40	91	2.98	4.29
2	73.76	77.93	47	30.92	34.48	92	2.76	3.94
3	72.79	76.95	48	30.02	33.56	93	2.56	3.61
4	71.81	75.96	49	29.13	32.65	94	2.38	3.29
5	70.82	74.98	50	28.23	31.74	95	2.21	3.02
6	69.84	73.99	51	27.34	30.85	96	2.06	2.79
7	68.85	73.00	52	26.46	29.96	97	1.91	2.61
8	67.87	72.02	53	25.58	29.08	98	1.77	2.43
9	66.88	71.03	54	24.72	28.21	99	1.64	2.23
10	65.90	70.05	55	23.86	27.34	100	1.53	2.03
11	64.91	69.06	56	23.02	26.49	101	1.42	1.84
12	63.93	68.08	57	22.19	25.65	102	1.32	1.66
13	62.95	67.10	58	21.37	24.82	103	1.23	1.49
14	61.98	66.12	59	20.55	23.99	104	1.13	1.33
15	61.01	65.14	60	19.75	23.18	105	1.04	1.19
16	60.05	64.17	61	18.96	22.37	106	0.95	1.05
17	59.10	63.19	62	18.18	21.58	107	0.86	0.93
18	58.15	62.22	63	17.42	20.79	108	0.78	0.82
19	57.21	61.25	64	16.67	20.01	109	0.70	0.72

20	56.26	60.27	65	15.94	19.24	110	0.62	0.63
21	55.32	59.30	66	15.23	18.48	111	0.55	0.56
22	54.37	58.33	67	14.53	17.73	112	0.47	0.48
23	53.43	57.36	68	13.84	16.99	113	0.40	0.42
24	52.48	56.39	69	13.16	16.27	114	0.34	0.34
25	51.54	55.42	70	12.50	15.55	115	0.27	0.28
26	50.60	54.45	71	11.84	14.84	116	0.21	0.22
27	49.65	53.48	72	11.20	14.15	117	0.16	0.16
28	48.71	52.51	73	10.59	13.48	118	0.10	0.11
29	47.77	51.55	74	9.99	12.81	119	0.05	0.06
30	46.82	50.58	75	9.40	12.16	120		
31	45.88	49.62	76	8.83	11.53			
32	44.93	48.65	77	8.28	10.91			
33	43.98	47.69	78	7.75	10.30			
34	43.03	46.73	79	7.25	9.72			
35	42.08	45.78	80	6.76	9.14			
36	41.14	44.82	81	6.30	8.59			
37	40.19	43.87	82	5.87	8.06			
38	39.25	42.92	83	5.45	7.55			
39	38.30	41.97	84	5.06	7.07			
40	37.36	41.03	85	4.69	6.60			
41	36.43	40.08	86	4.34	6.16			
42	35.50	39.14	87	4.02	5.74			
43	34.57	38.20	88	3.73	5.34			
44	33.65	37.26	89	3.45	4.98			

DEATHS PER 100,000 AT VARIOUS AGES

Center for Disease Control—United States Life Tables, 2003
Number Expected to Die Each Year

Age	Males Per 100,000	Females Per 100,000	Age	Males Per 100,000	Females Per 100,000	Age	Males Per 100,000	Females Per 100,000
0	761	608	34	154	84	67	1,665	1,203
1	51	41	35	167	96	68	1,754	1,288
2	36	29	36	181	102	69	1,897	1,369
3	29	22	37	193	112	70	2,000	1,524
4	22	17	38	204	119	71	2,073	1,590
5	19	14	39	224	132	72	2,249	1,719
6	17	13	40	242	148	73	2,355	1,827
7	15	13	41	266	159	74	2,459	1,963
8	16	12	42	289	174	75	2,633	2,101
9	14	13	43	306	182	76	2,746	2,254
10	18	14	44	338	206	77	2,833	2,417
11	16	13	45	355	219	78	2,912	2,534
12	22	13	46	401	240	79	3,023	2,705
13	25	16	47	429	251	80	3,140	2,908
14	33	17	48	457	267	81	3,174	3,031
15	43	24	49	495	291	82	3,155	3,160

16	70	35	50	530	311	83	3,348	3,433
17	90	39	51	562	333	84	3,070	3,325
18	120	49	52	602	363	85	3,029	3,409
19	134	46	53	614	375	86	2,957	3,465
20	137	48	54	688	423	87	2,853	3,488
21	139	48	55	710	445	88	2,720	3,476
22	142	50	56	802	509	89	2,558	3,424
23	136	49	57	771	507	90	2,371	3,332
24	134	51	58	891	600	91	2,163	3,197
25	130	49	59	968	650	92	1,940	3,023
26	133	54	60	1,070	725	93	1,709	2,812
27	128	56	61	1,091	735	94	1,476	2,570
28	127	54	62	1,225	836	95	1,248	2,303
29	133	61	63	1,274	888	96	1,031	2,022
30	135	62	64	1,376	982	97	832	1,735
31	137	66	65	1,452	1,034	98	654	1,453
32	147	68	66	1,547	1,105	99	500	1,185
33	146	78						

THE CHANCE OF DYING BEFORE AGE 65

From a group of 100,000 persons your age, the chart below illustrates the number who likely will still be alive at age 65. The third column indicates the probability that you will not be alive at age 65.

From 1,000 Males				From 1,000 Females		
Age at Last Birthday	Number Who Live To Age 65	Their Odds of Dying Before Age 65		Age at Last Birthday	Number Who Live To Age 65	Their Odds of Dying Before Age 65
30	840	16%		30	874	13%
31	840	16%		31	875	13%
32	842	16%		32	876	12%
33	843	16%		33	876	12%
34	844	16%		34	877	12%
35	845	16%		35	878	12%
36	846	15%		36	879	12%
37	848	15%		37	880	12%
38	849	15%		38	881	12%
39	850	15%		39	882	12%
40	852	15%		40	884	12%
41	853	15%		41	885	12%
42	855	15%		42	886	11%
43	857	14%		43	888	11%
44	859	14%		44	889	11%

Age	Value	%		Age	Value	%
45	862	14%		45	891	11%
46	864	14%		46	893	11%
47	867	13%		47	895	11%
48	870	13%		48	897	10%
49	874	13%		49	900	10%
50	877	12%		50	903	10%
51	881	12%		51	906	9%
52	885	12%		52	909	9%
53	890	11%		53	913	9%
54	895	11%		54	917	8%
55	900	10%		55	922	8%
56	906	9%		56	927	7%
57	913	8%		57	932	7%
58	921	8%		58	939	6%
59	929	7%		59	945	5%
60	939	6%		60	953	5%
61	948	5%		61	961	4%
62	959	4%		62	970	3%
63	971	3%		63	979	2%
64	985	2%		64	989	1%

Source: 2001 Commissioner's Standard Ordinary Mortality Table.

LIFE EXPECTANCY TABLE

Center for Disease Control—United States Life Tables, 2003

Life Expectancy In Years

Age	Male	Female	Age	Male	Female	Age	Male	Female
0	74.8	80.1	30	46.5	51.2	60	20.4	23.8
1	74.3	79.6	31	45.6	50.2	61	19.7	22.9
2	73.4	78.6	32	44.7	49.3	62	18.9	22.1
3	72.4	77.6	33	43.7	48.3	63	18.2	21.3
4	71.4	76.7	34	42.8	47.3	64	17.5	20.5
5	70.4	75.7	35	41.9	46.4	65	16.8	19.8
6	69.5	74.7	36	40.9	45.4	66	16.1	19.0
7	68.5	73.7	37	40.0	44.5	67	15.4	18.2
8	67.5	72.7	38	39.1	43.5	68	14.8	17.5
9	66.5	71.7	39	38.2	42.6	69	14.1	16.8
10	65.5	70.7	40	37.3	41.6	70	13.5	16.0
11	64.5	69.7	41	36.4	40.7	71	12.9	15.3
12	63.5	68.7	42	35.5	39.7	72	12.2	14.6
13	62.5	67.7	43	34.6	38.8	73	11.7	14.0
14	61.6	66.8	44	33.7	37.9	74	11.1	13.3
15	60.6	65.8	45	32.8	37.0	75	10.5	12.6
16	59.6	64.8	46	31.9	36.0	76	10.0	12.0

#			#			#		
17	58.6	63.8	47	31.1	35.1	77	9.5	11.4
18	57.7	62.8	48	30.2	34.2	78	9.0	10.8
19	56.8	61.9	49	29.3	33.3	79	8.5	10.2
20	55.8	60.9	50	28.5	32.4	80	8.0	9.6
21	54.9	59.9	51	27.7	31.5	81	7.6	9.1
22	54.0	58.9	52	26.8	30.6	82	7.2	8.6
23	53.1	58.0	53	26.0	29.7	83	6.7	8.1
24	52.1	57.0	54	25.2	28.9	84	6.4	7.6
25	51.2	56.0	55	24.4	28.0	85	6.0	7.2
26	50.3	55.1	56	23.6	27.1			
27	49.4	54.1	57	22.8	26.3			
28	48.4	53.1	58	22.0	25.4			
29	47.5	52.2	59	21.2	24.6			

CAVEATS

BOCA

Based on Current Assumptions

All figures are based on current assumptions of mortality, expense and interest; any change could affect the cash value, death benefit, and/or outlay as indicated on the proposal.

BOCT

Based on Current Taxes

All figures are based on current income and estate taxes. Any changes in the tax laws will impact this program, producing higher or lower after-tax yield.

BOLE

Based on Life Expectancy

All figures are based on current life expectancy. This term denotes a period in which the annuitant will be taxed on the interest alone. After such period, the annuitant will be taxed on the entire amount.

FAT-POLICY-THIN

The Most Insurance for The Least Money

Give the insurance company the least amount of money for the most insurance. Applicable only if you are sophisticated and understand you have left no margin for interest drop. Any rise in interest can make a thin policy fat and a fat policy obese.

A Checklist: Insuring Your Family's Future

There comes a time when every successful person must ask themselves difficult questions about life insurance. The answers could mean the difference between a comfortable life for your heirs or months of red tape and a substantial loss of money in estate taxes.

Smart Business spoke with Barry Kaye, professor at Florida Atlantic University and author of six books on life insurance and estate planning, about 15 questions regarding life insurance. Kaye said any no answer means you need help, insurance or an analysis of your present programs. Five no responses means you are losing money, not optimizing your assets and creating huge problems for your heirs or paying too much for your insurance.

1. **Have you arranged to pay your estate taxes at an effective discount using insurance?**

   Insurance on an annual basis or a single payment will always cost less than the actual estate tax.

2. **Do you know if you are paying too much for your current life insurance?**

   Because of improved mortality tables, as well as a new creative product, many policies are antiquated and much money can be saved.

3. Have you analyzed whether you are paying the lowest cost for your life insurance?

Any simple analysis will prove in black and white whether you are overpaying or not.

4. Are you borrowing your premiums and paying interest, which is less than the actual premiums itself?

A simple program of borrowing and paying annual interest in many situations will be less expensive than paying the actual premium itself.

5. Have you checked whether you have any antiquated policies that you no longer need?

These policies are now saleable in the secondary market, which can pay you cash substantially in excess of the existing cash value.

6. Have you analyzed whether it would be cheaper to buy last-to-die insurance or insurance on your spouse?

You may be paying too much on your own life and it may be more reasonable to use your spouse or purchase last-to-die insurance if it will do the same job at less cost.

7. Have you analyzed whether it would be more efficient to give gifts to charity by utilizing insurance instead of your own assets?

Money given to charity at death is always subject to where your stock and real estate portfolios may be. A life insurance policy owned by a charity guarantees they will receive what you want them to and at less cost.

8. Have you analyzed whether your older policies can be improved?

Many of the older policies have substantial cash values, which can be used with new policies to bring the annual costs below the current policy's premium.

9. Have you analyzed your IRA and pension and learned how to optimize them up to 50 times at your death?

If you do not need your IRA to support you, then you can effectively escape double taxation by making a distribution and purchasing life insurance on an income and estate tax free basis, which will produce at death a much greater return than your IRA.

10. Have you arranged to avoid the havoc at your death caused after 30 years of marriage with an unintentional antiquated prenuptial agreement no longer applicable?

Is it possible that the nature of your relationship has changed and the number of years involved would properly take your marriage to a different level to where you really wanted to take care of your spouse in a better way?

11. Have you analyzed whether you can give your unneeded social security to charity at many times its existing value?

If you don't need social security to live on, then avoid income taxes by giving the annual money to charity, which in turn will purchase a policy on your lives to create a much greater return.

12. **Do you really believe your advisors have given you the best up-to-date solution to your situation?**

Have things changed since your original advice and is it possible that you can create superior approaches for your objectives?

13. **Do you believe your estate plan needs a second opinion?**

Most anything of importance should always require a second opinion.

14. **Do you realize the time spent on your estate planning is small by comparison to the large effect on your family forever?**

Whatever you do or don't do will provide the consequences that will impact the people closest to you for a long time to come.

15. **Do you really want to ruin a 30-year relationship at death by the consequences of your action or inaction?**

You are so highly thought of that it is inappropriate to spoil these opinions and leave the wrong legacy behind.

© 2006 *Smart Business Network Inc.* Reprinted from the August 2006 issue of *Smart Business Broward/Palm Beach*.

About the Author

A native New Yorker who began his career as a radio and TV personality, Barry Kaye joined New England Life as an insurance agent in 1962 and proceeded to break all life insurance industry sales records in his first year.

In 1966, he received his CLU degree from The American College in Bryn Mawr, Pennsylvania. Soon after, Kaye was named a lifetime member of the Million-Dollar Round Table Club, and became one of the founders of the prestigious International Forum.

He established Barry Kaye Associates, a national firm headquartered in Los Angeles, in 1968. His innovative uses of life insurance earned him a reputation for creativity in the insurance field, and his outstanding integrity and financial acumen resulted in astonishing success in his field. He has led fifteen life insurance companies during his career. He was the catalyst for last-to-die life insurance in 1963 and in 2002 originated the concept of life expectancy insurance policies.

Kaye is the prolific author of eight books and several videos on the subjects of life insurance and estate planning. His first book, *How to Save a Fortune on Your Life Insurance*, an immediate best seller, was instrumental in accelerating a lower pricing structure for life insurance. His next book and videotape, *Save a Fortune on Your Estate Taxes* (Forman Publishing, Inc.), was also a top-seller. His third book,

Die Rich and Tax Free! (Forman Publishing, Inc.) presented his ideas in an easy to follow chart format. In *Live Rich* (Dove Books), Kaye shares the techniques and philosophies he has employed throughout his lifetime to achieve financial success and a deeply rewarding lifestyle for himself and his family. *The Investment Alternative* (Forman Publishing, Inc.) was the first book to show that life insurance was not an expense but rather an asset. In 2000 he wrote *Die Rich 2* (FHA Press), the first financial book of the millennium. He has appeared twice on NBC's *Today* show.

Barry Kaye, who is listed in *Who's Who in America, Who's Who in the West* and *Who's Who in Finance and Industry,* has served on the California Senate Advisory Commission on Life Insurance. A philanthropist, he has contributed $1,000,000 to the CLU College; he is a member of the Board of Ben Gurion University and the City of Hope; one of the founders of La Societe and the Los Angeles Music Center and former vice chairman of the Young Musicians' Foundation.

The author is the recipient of the Man of Hope award from the City of Hope for Founders of Diabetic Research (1976), the Menachim Begin Award for Israel Bonds (1977) and the Lifetime Achievement Award from Ben Gurion University of the Negev (1987).

He recently made a generous donation to enhance The Carole and Barry Kaye Performing Arts Auditorium on the Florida Atlantic University (FAU) campus. In addition, Barry Kaye donated $5 million to FAU, with a matching grant from the state of Florida that should bring it up to $10 million, for the establishment of the "Barry Kaye School of Finance, Insurance, and Economics in the College of Business," as well as the "Barry Kaye Institute of Insurance in Philanthropy." The school will bring together the major academic and professional components of the financial services industry. Barry Kaye was also granted an honorary doctoral degree from FAU as well as a professorship, and a senior faculty position that will provide academic leadership in the field of insurance and financial planning.

Barry Kaye received the coveted Financial Advisor of the Year award from Financial Services Advisor Magazine in 1999. He was the fourth winner of this award; the three previous winners were Sir Harry Templeton, Peter Lynch and Warren Buffett. In 2002, Barry Kaye was Man-of-the-Year for the Anti-Defamation League, Jewish Federation of Palm Beach County and Chairman of the Love and Hope Ball for the Institute for Diabetic Research at the University of Miami.

Over the last two years Barry Kaye won the silver and gold award for the Jerry Lewis Muscular Dystrophy Telethon, raising the most money in a 10-minute segment. In 2005 Mr. Kaye raised $50,000 from the public and matched with gifts of $50,000 of his own for the MDA and an additional $50,000 for the Katrina Fund. In 2006 Mr. Kaye again raised $50,000 on a matching gifts program on the telethon and raised $50,000 from the public and $50,000 of his own.

Contact Information

If you would like more information about any concept discussed in this book, please contact my office at:

Barry Kaye Associates
5100 Town Center Circle, Suite 550
Boca Raton, Florida 33486
(561) 417-5883
(561) 417-3558 - Fax
(800) DIE RICH – (800) 343-7424 Toll Free
http://www.barrykaye.com